VICTORIAN
Costume for Ladies
1860-1900

Linda Setnik

Schiffer Publishing Ltd

4880 Lower Valley Road, Atglen, PA 19310 USA

A Note on the Photographs

To aid the reader in identification and dating, many photographs are presented with their card stock intact. "TS" refers to the presence of a tax stamp. Captions include the location of the photographer to illustrate that styles differed little from one section of the country to another. "NM" indicates that no photographer's mark and/or location were shown on the picture.

Library of Congress Cataloging-in-Publication Data

Setnik, Linda.
Victorian costumes for ladies, 1860-1900 / Linda Setnik.
p. cm.
Includes bibliographical references and index.
ISBN 0-7643-1054-2 (pbk.)
1. Costume--History--19th century. 2. Costumes--Great Britain--History--19th century.
I. Title.
GT737.S47 2000
391'.2'097309034--dc21
99-056993

Designed by Bonnie M. Hensley
Type set in BernhardMod BT/Lydian BT

ISBN: 0-7643-1054-2
Printed in China
1 2 3 4

Published by Schiffer Publishing Ltd.
4880 Lower Valley Road
Atglen, PA 19310
Phone: (610) 593-1777; Fax: (610) 593-2002
E-mail: Schifferbk@aol.com
Please visit our web site catalog at **www.schifferbooks.com**

In Europe, Schiffer books are distributed by Bushwood Books
6 Marksbury Avenue Kew Gardens
Surrey TW9 4JF England
Phone: 44 (0)208-392-8585; Fax: 44 (0)208-392-9876
E-mail: Bushwd@aol.com
Free postage in the UK. Europe: air mail at cost.

This book may be purchased from the publisher.
Include $3.95 for shipping. Please try your bookstore first.
We are interested in hearing from authors with book ideas on related subjects.
You may write for a free printed catalog.

Dedication

This book is dedicated to my husband, Bob, whose patience, encouragement, and continued faith in my abilities helped me produce the following work.

Acknowledgments

I would like to thank Joan Henry of Sierra West Booksellers and Carl Mautz of Carl Mautz Vintage Photographs for their wonderful selection of photographs, many of which appear within the pages of this book and enabled me to include such thorough coverage for each time period. A special thanks to Joan for also having collected so many terrific old books and fashion magazines. The staff at the Fair Oaks Library deserves recognition for their efforts in acquiring the microfilm for over thirty years of Godey's Lady's Book and for cheerfully keeping the antiquated microfiche machine in working order! My editor, Jennifer Lindbeck, was much appreciated for her patience and encouragement. I want to thank my daughter, Jennie Cunningham, and my parents, Murle and Dolly Klohs, for all their love and support throughout the years. My sister Wendy's and my mother- and father-in-law Alyce and Harry's kindness and words of encouragement were greatly valued. I would also like to express my appreciation to God for pointing me in the right direction and enabling me to find just the right photograph or information.

Contents

Introduction _____ 6

PART I: General Topics _____ 8

Chapter 1: Undergarments _____ 9
Chapter 2: Casual Wear _____ 12
Chapter 3: Sports Clothes _____ 14
Chapter 4: Common Dress _____ 18
Chapter 5: Evening Attire _____ 20
Chapter 6: Clothing Manufacture _____ 34
Chapter 7: Laundry _____ 36
Chapter 8: Personal Hygiene _____ 38
Chapter 9: Cosmetics _____ 40

PART II: Ladies' Daytime Street Apparel _____ 42

Chapter 10: 1860-1864 _____ 43
Chapter 11: 1865-1868 _____ 58
Chapter 12: 1869-1875 _____ 72
Chapter 13: 1876-1878 _____ 86
Chapter 14: 1879-1882 _____ 100
Chapter 15: 1883-1888 _____ 118
Chapter 16: 1889-1892 _____ 132
Chapter 17: 1893-1896 _____ 142
Chapter 18: 1897-1900 _____ 152

Appendix: Dating the Victorian Paper Photograph _____ 162
Price Guide _____ 172
Bibliography _____ 174
Index _____ 176

ntroduction

Clothing played a major role in the everyday lives of Victorian women. Fashion was a tyrant few dared disobey. Among her many dictates was the demand that outfits be suited to the occasion. Appropriate dress varied with the task and the time of day, requiring women to change clothes frequently. The sheer number of under and outer garments made the simple act of dressing a complicated and time-consuming process. The lack of ready-made clothes through much of the period insured numerous visits to the dressmaker or, for those less fortunate, many tedious hours aiding the seamstress or working alone to fabricate the families' clothing. Renovating costly, outmoded outfits to ensure their conformance with current styles involved additional hours. Intricate costumes also required considerable maintenance to lengthen the interval between the grueling process of laundering. Realizing the influence of appropriate apparel upon social acceptance and not wishing to be outdone by their neighbors, most women, despite personal finances, spent considerable time and money to insure a proper wardrobe.

Far from being frivolous, the study of clothing is vital to a complete understanding of women's social history during the Victorian period. Having a passion for all aspects of the American Victorian era, my interest in period clothing intensified with my growing collection of nineteenth-century photographs. To more precisely date the costumes depicted, I began extensive research using available books on the topic. Amazingly, I discovered that the information necessary to categorize each period of clothing simply and accurately did not exist. And not only did I wish to date the outfits—I wanted a better understanding of the impact such elaborate and restrictive clothing had upon the lives of our Victorian ancestors.

Confronted with a baffling assortment of conflicting information, it became clear I would have to unearth primary sources to unlock the secrets of the past. I began by collecting fashion periodicals, along with requesting from the local library microfilm copies of the premier Victorian fashion magazine, *Godey's Lady's Book*. (These not only feature fashion plates but enlightening and invaluable commentary on how the Victorian's viewed the latest styles.) To gain further insight into the period, I supplemented my existing library with additional nineteenth-century medical, etiquette, beauty, home, and architectural books. Along with my extensive collection of Victorian photographs—each of which I have examined minutely with a ten-power loop—the aggregate provided a thorough understanding of the costumes and their relationship to the era created. Taking my cues directly from period documents, I let them guide me through the labyrinth of fashion.

Costume changed frequently throughout the Victorian period (1837-1901). While the book spans the four decades corresponding to paper portraiture photography (1860-1900), clothing is divided into nine sections whose dates reflect the significant stylistic changes unique to each four- to seven-year time span. Women's clothing and foundations are clearly explained, along with the mental, physical, and social aspects related to wearing such complex, restrictive garments. Hairstyles and jewelry are included, as each changed with the styles and forms a crucial part in the complete visualization of the Victorian woman. The bulk of the book focuses on women's street wear, with additional chapters exploring evening and casual, at-home gowns, along with related subjects like clothing manufacture, laundry, and personal hygiene. Frequently overlooked in contemporary literature, these and other topics are separated from the rest of the text to maintain cohesiveness and facilitate comprehension. Combined with the detailed account of ladies' fashions, the aggregate provides knowledge not only of period costume but of what it was like to fabricate, wear, and maintain such intricate garments.

A minimum of thirty photographs accompany each chapter to illustrate the written prose and provide irrefutable documentation of the outfits. While fashion plates are helpful as a dating guide, they often exaggerated details and can prove misleading when used to envision garments worn by the average woman. Surviving period clothing has frequently been altered and lacks the accessories and finesse bestowed by the original owner. Both lack the authenticity and realism that period photographs alone can convey.

Photography studios were almost as up to date in their furnishings as ladies were in their fashions. Careful study of photographs reveals exactly what furniture styles (especially in tables and chairs) were popular during each period, greatly aiding furniture collectors and dealers in dating their antiques.

Along with imparting a true picture of the era for theatrical purposes, fashions are important from a historical context, for wherever women's clothing is discernible, pictures can generally be dated within a five-year context. A knowledge of both fashion and nineteenth-century photography enabled me to identify minute differences in card stock and studio settings from one period to the next. The book closes with an appendix devoted to the identification and dating of photographs based on their format and images. To aid the reader in this classification process, many photos are presented throughout the book with their card stock intact. Used alone or coupled with a knowledge of women's ever-changing clothing, the information aids in accurately dating historic as well as family photographs.

My intent was to break through the bewildering realm of Victorian fashion and write a book that was concise, comprehensive, and understandable. Please join me in a fact-based journey through the fascinating world of Victorian fashion.

Part I

General Topics

No heathen god or goddess has ever had more zealous devotees than fashion, or a more absurd and humiliating ritual, or more mortifying and cruel penances. Her laws, like those of the Medes and Persions, must be implicitly obeyed, but unlike them, change, as certainly as the moon. They are rarely founded in reason, usually violate common sense, sometimes common decency, and uniformly common comfort. Fashion rules the world, and a most tyrannical mistress she is—compelling people to submit to the most inconvenient things imaginable for her sake. . . . She imposes unanticipated burdens, without regard to the strength or means of her hood-winked followers, cheating them out of time, fortune and happiness . . . If she fancies comparative nakedness for winter, or five thicknesses of woolen for dog days— she speaks, and it is done. If she orders the purple current of life and the organs of respiration to be retarded by steel, whalebone, buckram, drill, and cords—it is done. Disease laughs and death grins at the folly of the goddess and the zeal of the worshipers. . . . Abused women generally outlive fashionable ones. . . . The reason is plain: fashion kills more women than toil and sorrow. Obedience to fashion is a greater transgression of the laws of woman's nature, a greater injury to her physical and mental constitution, than the hardships of poverty and neglect.

The Royal Path of Life, 1879

Chapter One

Undergarments

Physical laws [are] perpetually broken by an established and unvarying style of senseless underwear, which has been handed down from generation to generation, and which we have all accepted from our mothers and grandmothers as the legacy of Fate, asking no questions as to its utility, and dreaming of nothing else as possible.

(Dress Reform, 1874)

Many a school-girl, whose waist was originally of a proper and healthful size, has gradually pressed the soft bones of youth until the lower ribs that should rise and fall with every breath, become entirely unused. Then the abdominal breathing, performed by the lower part of the lungs, ceases; the whole system becomes reduced in strength; the abdominal muscles that hold up the interior organs become weak, and the upper ones gradually sink upon the lower.

(American Woman's Home, 1869)

No matter how loosely the corset is worn, the lungs cannot be filled completely while their lower portions are thus encased . . . . [muscles] are weakened, not strengthened, by any outside "support" furnished by the corset, because the pressure impairs the circulation, and the nourishment of the tissues. They become flabby, and their loss of power to support the organs is seen in countless displacements and diseases. Heavy skirts fastened about the waist drag downward the whole pelvic viscera; weakness and prolapsion is the result; in short, almost every known disease may be traced to heavy skirts and their ally—the corset.

(Vivilore, 1904)

Practicality and comfort had little impact upon clothing or the undergarments necessary to form whatever curves or bulges current fashion deemed necessary. Dress played an important role in an age that prized a ladylike demeanor and judged people largely according to outward appearance. Social acceptance depended upon the wearing of fashionable apparel, which in turn leaned heavily on the shaping and bolstering it received from the garments beneath. Little thought was given to altering these uncomfortably heavy, clumsy, or constricting underclothes. They were simply accepted as the normal inheritance of the female race, whose prior generations were known to have worn even more extreme superstructures, such as bust-flattening corsets or hip-enlarging panniers. Individualism was not a desired feminine trait during the Victorian Period, and even those so inclined seldom wished to risk public ridicule by rebelling against established practices.

Though denounced by physicians for a large list of possible injurious side effects, corsets were used throughout the period to encourage flesh to conform to the varying standards of beauty. Internal organs became cramped or displaced, resulting in assorted difficulties involving the reproductive, digestive, and respiratory systems. Nevertheless, corsets were deemed essential to reduce waist size. They also provided breast support and prevented unsightly bulges to insure a smooth line beneath snug-fitting clothing. Proponents at the time even believed they were necessary to help the weaker sex maintain adequate

posture—and women did come to depend upon this artificial support, their muscles weakened by continued compression since childhood. Indeed, flabby muscles became so accustomed to this manmade bracing that most women remained stubbornly oblivious to the corset's health risks, maintaining that they never tightened their own stays sufficiently to induce harm.

Vertical bands of whalebone originally stiffened corsets, though a preference for cane and steel emerged by the late seventies as increasingly tight lacing often caused the former to crack. Some included a long narrow "busk" down the center front to help hold the stomach firm. Corsets fit over the breasts, with special fabric insets called "gussets" accommodating fullness there and at the hips. For those less endowed, bust improvers or "pads" were promoted by the mid-seventies, stuffed with cork and later grass or hair-covered springs.

Corsets (also known as "stays") had front closures with laces in back to regulate size. Corset length and their degree of tightening fluctuated with the fashions. So prized was a tiny waist that the molding thereof began almost at birth. Modified corsets were available for toddlers and small children, complete with attachments to hold diapers or stockings. By the age of thirteen, adolescents' stays generally resembled those worn by adults. Though diminutive waist measurements may have referred to corset circumference rather than actual waist size—as stays did not meet at the back but allowed two to four inches for lacing—tiny waistlines were nonetheless a reality upon the slender frames of women whose height averaged little more than five feet. Nineteenth-century physicians attested that relentless compression of the mid-section since childhood caused ribs and vital organs to contract and flesh to recede accordingly. The extent of the resulting deformity corresponded to the degree of tightening—with some women being more exuberant in their adherence to the dictates of fashion than others.

Stays were not only available for all age groups but in numerous styles (at least for adults) to suit individual needs. Some came equipped with shoulder straps to provide extra support. Less constricting stays allowed women more freedom of movement while attending to their toilet or household chores. Specially-made corsets with breast flaps permitted new mothers to retain the use of that indispensable article even while nursing. "Skeleton" and "Ventilated" models offered cooler summer alternatives by the seventies, along with "healthful" styles that continued to expand their offerings in each successive decade and allegedly possessed greater pliability for extra comfort and freedom of movement. Eighteen-eighties corsets featured abdominal laces to afford pregnant women expansion where they needed it most (as the use of stays during the first five or six months of gestation was common—their removal or loose application sufficing afterward!). Advertisements for waist-length versions appeared by the last decade of the century, promising exceptional flexibility for the growing numbers of health-conscious individuals actively participating in sports.

"Chemises" were worn underneath expensive corsets to protect them from soiling and to prevent delicate skin from becoming chaffed or pinched by tight lacing. Chemises were loose, low-necked, knee-length garments. Corset covers (or "camisoles") were worn over stays to help soften the rigid lines of boning and shield the dress lining from perspiration. Also low necked, they extended to the hips and were shaped to the figure, closing with buttons at the front. (Occasionally the chemise contained an additional flap of fabric that extended over the corset, eliminating the need for a separate covering.) Both garments had short sleeves (with sleeveless versions available by the seventies) that, along with the neckline, the women and young ladies of the household often embellished with elaborate embroidery.

Though the sleeves of the chemise and camisole provided some protection from underarm clothing stains, dress shields made from buckskin and later rubber were advertised by the early seventies (and may have existed in homemade versions before that time). These were a great boon in preventing costly undergarments and bodices from being destroyed by stains and odor, as effective deodorants were unfortunately not one of the many "preparations" available during the Victorian era. Small detachable cuffs or the larger undersleeves, as well as detachable collars, were also beneficial in extending the life of outer garments.

While corsets reduced the waistline, hoops and bustles provided an illusion of excess flesh; all were equally ridiculed for disfiguring rather than flattering the natural curves of the anatomy. "Bustles" (or "tournures"), intermittently popular from 1869 to 1888, and the hoops that dominated the 1860s (also called "crinolines" after the horsehair petticoat they replaced in 1856) were made in varying shapes and sizes to fit current dress styles. Hoops were formed from progressively-expanding, circular-shaped "watch spring" steel, which fit within the casings of a petticoat or attached to vertical tapes radiating from a waistband. The combination was both strong and pliable, allowing the unwieldy garment to accommodate the wearer as much as possible while sitting or navigating. Though cumbersome and sometimes even dangerous, catching onto objects or coming in too close proximity with stoves or fireplaces, many women appreciated the hoop for being lighter and cooler than the numerous petticoats it replaced. Bustles required fullness only in back, and shaped hoops were quickly reduced to semicircular steels similarly held within tapes or petticoats. Alternate versions were available shed of their useless front halves, with the remaining portion secured simply by ties about the waist. These coexisted with even lighter, half-length "crinolettes," which also fastened around the waist and could be formed of curved steels or horsehair padding; many were collapsible, affording greater comfort to the wearer while sitting. In spite of efforts to reduce bulk, bustles continued to support the uneven distribution of heavy fabrics, which threw the body out of alignment and caused innumerable back problems. Even when full-blown bustles were not in vogue, modified steels or shallow pads were generally available options.

Petticoats of varying numbers were worn over hoops and bustles or on their own when these had lost favor. Differing degrees and levels of starched flounces, placed around the entire circumference or only at the bottom or back, augmented petticoats to emphasize the figure according to prevailing fashion. When trains were only in vogue for evenings, an "adjustable train" that fastened to the petticoat's back lengths could make a single undergarment serviceable for both day and evening. During the winter months, flannel petticoats might be worn beneath hoops and bustles for added warmth and protection from cold drafts. The weight of these long, full petticoats combined with dress skirts (which were often accompanied by overskirts and trains) to tax the strength of the wearer, not only in strenuous pursuits but in the simple act of locomotion!

The underpants worn beneath voluminous petticoats were just beginning to be viewed as necessary rather than optional apparel. Though introduced shortly after the turn of the century, women were slow to adopt this previously-masculine apparel. "Pantalets" were reserved mostly for children. Fancy ankle and later calf-length versions trimmed at the bottom with ruffles or lace were commonly found exposed beneath the shorter skirts of young girls. These were generally discarded at the age of fifteen or sixteen, presumably because the newly-donned, floor-length dresses, along with the long chemise and numerous petticoats, were considered adequate covering. It was not until the hoop eliminated the need for excessive petticoats and made accidental observances more plausible that the plainer, below-the-knee length "drawers" became more prevalent. Both styles were left open at the crotch for convenience and, in common with other undergarments, were seldom colored, as the recent artificial clothing dyes were frequently made from poisonous substances.

By the late seventies, petticoats united with corset covers, and drawers combined with a narrowed chemise to form "union suits" (an innovation promoted briefly in the late fifties for travel or boarding). Both became popular alternatives to help eliminate bulk and render a smooth fit beneath the tight dresses then in vogue. They also provided much-needed relief around the midriff, for the broad waistbands of standard undergarments and outer clothing were necessarily doubled for strength. Ten or more layers of fabric pressing tightly against the waist were common, causing discomfort and making corsets almost a necessity to compensate for the accumulated thicknesses. Combination undergarments also helped distribute excessive fabric weight from the hips to the shoulders, easing the strain (and possible health risks) from the abdomen and rendering the "skirt suspenders" of the late sixties less of a necessity.

To add to the already burdensome number of undergarments, the medical profession proclaimed the necessity for an insulating layer of flannel against the torso to regulate body temperature. This covering was intended for summer and winter in locals with a significant temperature variance or when one was in danger of catching a chill after becoming overheated. (Such incidences were said to force the flow of blood inward, resulting in an overabundance to certain regions—believed a prime factor in many diseases.) When confronted with questionable or even established benefits to her health, the Victorian woman generally shunned such sage advice in deference to what was fashionable or would maintain her slender physique.

Long cotton, knit, or silk stockings completed the requisite undergarments. Elastic garters sufficiently tight to suspend them above or below the knees also restricted blood flow, causing cramps or numbness. To help alleviate this problem a few corsets came equipped with stocking attachments, and separate "stocking" or "hose supporters" resembling garter belts were marketed by the seventies. These contained two long straps, one resting along the outside of each thigh, which further branched into two clips to grasp the stocking's upper edge. Though these were less constricting, some ladies continued to prefer the standard garters. A supply of hose (as well as drawers and other undergarments) sufficient for two changes a week in summer and one in winter was believed ample.

Chapter Two

Casual Wear

How many women go about their houses, daily, in untidy toilet, and at night the tired husband sees the same loose wrapper and unsmoothed hair that he parted with at breakfast, unless some uninterested visitor should happen to have called, and then, for their sake, the wife is freshly and becomingly attired.

(Demorist's, April 1876)

A wrapper made with handsome trimming, open over a pretty white skirt, may be worn with propriety; but the simple dress worn for breakfast, or in the exercise of domestic duties, is not suitable for the parlor when receiving visits of ceremony in the morning.

(The Ladies' Book of Etiquette, 1873)

The careful woman never lounges in a handsome and carefully fitted street gown. She wears a house dress indoors, and when she desires to rest in her room she dons a dressing sack.

(Delineator, October 1893)

Informal, at-home attire during the Victorian period became synonymous with the wrapper: an unpretentious garment that allowed women some freedom from the normal constraints of fashion while they attended to household affairs. Wrappers were constructed from less-expensive printed cotton fabrics such as chintz, gingham, and calico—with wool used for warmth during the winter months. Less constricting "morning corsets" were intended for wear beneath, as apparently were hoops and bustles (or at the least, numerous petticoats). Wrappers that appeared to fit loose were deceptive, as most incorporated a snug, front-fastening inner lining that attached to the side seams and extended to the waist or hips. While not exactly leisure wear, wrappers were more comfortable than standard street apparel and far more practical, for they were made from lightweight, affordable fabrics that lacked overskirts or excessive trim and were easier to construct, launder, and iron.

Usually one-piece (with a few two-piece styles introduced in the eighties), long-sleeved, and covering at least to the base of the neck, wrappers could assume various styles depending on the period. Most fell within three categories: yoked on the bodice and gathered from there to fall loose or, more likely, be girded by a belt (known as the "Mother Hubbard"); seamed and darted to fit closer at the waist in the more elegant, one-piece princess style; or fitted in front and hanging loose or "sacque style" in back, with extra fabric box-pleated at the neck and falling straight down in "Wateau fashion." Outfits closed in front with buttons extending anywhere from the hips to the floor and might be plain or simply decorated with a ruffle along the hem. Sleeve styles and skirt fullness followed current fashions. If trains were common upon daytime street wear, they also adorned wrappers. Though a nuisance, trains lent a graceful, dignified appearance and were far more practical sweeping upon clean floors and carpets or manicured lawns than dusty streets.

The versatile, full-bodied wrapper proved an ideal maternity garment as it allowed abundant expansion to the expectant mother who, not wishing to publicize her "condition" unduly, was generally homebound toward the end of her pregnancy. While standard day wear worn with corsets was permissible before this time, by the seventh month of gestation stays were to be set aside or worn loosely—but so attached were women to this article that medical books sometimes had to specify their removal during labor! Clothing expressly constructed for maternity would not become available until after the turn of the century, though loose tunics and skirts supplemented with drawstring waists occasionally sufficed.

With the possible exception of the frontier, the wrapper was considered proper for home use around family members only, to be worn in the mornings while breakfasting and attending to domestic duties. (This stricture would not ease until the nineties, when wrappers were finally more accepted for the street—as long as they were properly belted.) Aprons were necessary adjuncts to protect fabric and lessen the need for frequent washing. By noon (the hour when formal "morning" visits actually began) ladies were supposed to be properly attired. Though this rule of etiquette was frequently ignored when guests were not expected, it was considered just as important to present a pleasing appearance to family members. "Proper attire" consisted of "house dresses," which were periodically illustrated in fashion magazines and usually resembled a simplified, though often gayer and more brightly hued, version of street attire. The finer clothing was thus kept in pristine condition for display while promenading and visiting acquaintances or, more especially, carriage riding (where mud could not infringe upon trains and elegant fabrics). Less wear also insured greater longevity to the more expensive outfits, which were so difficult to fabricate and equally hard to launder and maintain. The shirtwaist, whose suitability for street wear fluctuated, was usually considered an acceptable supplement to the house dress. By the 1870s, elaborate princess versions of the wrapper, often labeled "tea gowns," appeared in fine fabrics such as silk or velvet, beautifully trimmed with lace and ribbon, and these too were deemed suitable—even as hostess wear for informal, afternoon tea parties. By dinnertime, however, more dignified attire replaced the less decorous gown.

The articles providing the greatest comfort for wear indoors were variously named "dressing sacks," "combing mantles," "breakfast jackets," and "matinees." All featured a loose fit, front closure, and complete coverage from neck to thigh. Usually quite feminine and frilly, ornamented with ruffles and lace, they combined with a simple flounced or ruffled skirt (or with a dress skirt left over from a former season) to form a "negligee toilette." While hoops and bustles were not required, special "negligee corsets" were advertised. The presence or absence of a belt was important. When worn loose, they were only deemed appropriate in private chambers for lounging or attending to the hair and makeup, whereas belted and accompanied by a "morning cap," they could be presented with propriety at the breakfast table. Similar garments could also be worn in the evenings before retiring, along with long, robe-like "sack night dresses" or "night wrappers" (not to be confused with the flowing "night gowns," which also covered the body from head to foot and were intended as sleep wear).

Two sisters wear identical wrappers with double flounces at the hem; long sleeves with short, full oversleeves; turn-down collars; bretelles. c. 1893. Mt. Carmel, Illinois.

Mid-nineties yoked wrapper. Bodice droops low center front and has full, leg-of-mutton sleeves. Council Bluffs, Iowa.

Two young ladies standing to rear of photo wear simple yoked, late-nineties wrappers. NM

Chapter Three

Sports Clothes

If young ladies ride on horseback for exercise . . . what does it avail them, pinched and burdened as they are by their dress? If they row, it is under like conditions; and the results are the same.

(Dress Reform, 1874)

It is not a simple matter to effect abrupt and radical changes in customs that have prevailed for ages, and many women cyclists, therefore, cling to the essentially feminine skirt . . . Those who adopt reforms readily have welcomed the new bloomers or trousers as a most practical innovation, and so rapidly has this fashion grown in favor that the so-called "rational dress" is now worn without provoking comment.

(Delineator, April 1895)

She who was all grace and loveliness in her rustling silks and flashing diamonds, is commonplace and almost ridiculous in her limp and dripping bloomer robes as she emerges from the surf . . .

(Godey's, June 1875)

The luxury of comfortable clothing was only permissible indoors throughout most of the Victorian era. Women wore basically the same attire for many outdoor activities as they did for street wear. For sports like croquet and ice-skating, as well as activities popular during the last quarter of the century such as archery, boating, or lawn tennis, little accommodation was made other than appropriate footwear, perhaps accompanied by skirts shortened to ankle length. These modifications generally sufficed for people accustomed to wearing burdensome clothing in their daily lives. Attractive garments were also appreciated for the picturesque effect they lent to the overall scenery. Even the articles worn by women engaged in wilderness activities like camping, hiking, and mountain-climbing differed little from standard street attire. In fact, ladies were urged to wear their older clothing, as long as it was still stylish!

Some adaptation did exist for horseback riding, where ladies were at least unencumbered by hoops, bustles, fancy overskirts, back-drapery, or excess trim. Side-saddled riders were engulfed in floor-length skirts, however (many with trains), along with slim-fitting basques that required the expertise of tailors for strength as well as a perfect, body-molding fit. Though amply covered, weights were enclosed within skirt hems as extra protection against accidental exposure of the limbs. Often two long skirts were worn so that one could be disengaged if necessary while still allowing the rider to remain properly clothed. This precaution was no longer necessary by the seventies, when slim-fitting trousers complete with straps at the instep provided ample coverage beneath. The nineties offered bouffant divided skirts similar to those worn for bicycle riding (some with flap fronts), allowing the truly liberated woman the luxury of riding astride while retaining a sem-

blance of modesty. Corsets were requisite, though extreme lacing was discouraged.

While riding was generally reserved for the wealthier classes, the more affordable sport of bicycling blossomed into a national pastime by the mid-nineties, when it was readily accepted by a populace sufficiently enlightened about the health benefits of physical exercise. Though early tricyclists from the mid-eighties donned their long skirts and bustles, the first practical active wear soon emerged to meet the needs of this growing entertainment. Named after Amelia Bloomer, they bore little resemblance to the original 1850s ensemble, which consisted of Turkish or masculine-style trousers worn with calf-length dresses. Initially intended to offer women less restrictive street clothing, early garments deviated too drastically from everyday attire, limiting their adoption over the years to a few radical "dress reformers." Spurred by safety reasons, as long skirts could become entangled within the spokes or pedals of the increasingly-popular, two-wheeled bicycles, the now-bouffant, universally close-ankle bloomer resurfaced. Believed far less modest than skirts, the style was adopted with considerable trepidation. The not-unfounded fear also arose that bloomers would initiate the ultimate demise of the full rustling skirt, long a symbol of femininity. While embraced by the daring, more timid constitutions were given other, less drastic alternatives. Bloomers might be covered by floor-length overskirts, which were raised by drawstrings to hip level while riding and then quickly released upon dismount. Or, full-length divided "skirts" were available. These were indistinguishable from the standard article until the elastic hidden within casings near the ankles was pulled taught, causing each section to form about the leg in imitation of bloomers (this style was also recommended for mountain climbing and horseback riding). Stockings or leggings, sturdy shoes, cap, jacket, and the shirtwaist (which allowed freer movement and had appeared during the late eighties for sports such as tennis or croquet) completed the outer garments. Underneath, some enthusiasts were bold enough to suggest complete removal of the corset, though most opted for the new, less radical, waist-length versions. While such attire might have provided a semblance of comfort, full-length woolen union suits were recommended beneath for summer as well as winter to absorb perspiration and protect against the life-threatening chill that might otherwise result from becoming overheated.

If turn-of-the-century America had difficulty accepting the bloomer, the donning of beach wear in the sixties must truly have elicited concern. Not only was modesty in jeopardy, as bathing was the only public display that left women totally bereft of the many layers of finery that afforded such ladylike essence to her normal everyday appearance. Though early-sixties tunic and trouser ensembles covered the wearer from head to foot, attire from later in the decade, while far from revealing, nevertheless exposed arms below short puffed sleeves and revealed shapely, stocking-covered ankles. By the eighties, sleeveless, calf-length versions were available—though the remainder of the body remained hidden beneath loose full trousers and belted over-dresses, which had slowly risen from the knees to thighs. Although the short puffed sleeves of the nineties again hid the upper arms, some styles were so risque they displayed knees beneath short tunics that entirely covered the drawers underneath. Thin fabrics were shunned in favor of heavy, dark-colored flannels, which were less figure-revealing when wet, and weights were often sewn into hems to prevent skirts from escalating in a breeze or floating to the surface of the water. Along with slippers, dark-colored stockings, and the ubiquitous corset, all combined to provide adequate protection to feminine modesty—with the downside that the aggregate weight made swimming so dangerous, wading was all women dared with any degree of safety. An oil skin cap to protect hair from the harsh salt water provided the crowning glory.

Elegant, early-sixties riding costume. NM

Precursor to the nineties bicycling costume, this lady from the early sixties wears an inelegant bloomer reform outfit intended for street wear: long trousers; knee-length, one-piece Gabrielle dress. New York, New York.

A full-blown bloomer costume is shown in this mid-nineties stereo card, which mocks
women's newfound independence achieved with the bicycle. Caption reads, "Have
lunch ready at one, Charley."

Opposite Page

Two young ladies with stocking-covered legs and knee-
length bathing costumes. Los Angeles, California.
Photo hand dated "August, 1892."

Chapter Four

Common Dress

There are few lines of dress demarcation here [in America] to distinguish mistress from maid; and while the one enjoys a large share of favor, based, it may be, wholly upon externals, is it any wonder that the other apes her, even though it prove a hard-earned folly?

(Dress Reform, 1874)

Young women who neglect their toilet and manifest little concern about dress, indicate a general disregard of order—a mind but ill adapted to the details of housekeeping—a deficiency of taste and of the qualities that inspire love.

(Decorum, 1877)

Our purpose is to show that stylish and beautiful costumes cost no more than vulgar-looking ones, and that it is taste, not money, that makes the well-dressed lady. Hence we give the latest Parisian fashions, not only in all their entirety, in our colored plates, but adapted, in our "Every-Day" department, to the cheapest and most ordinary materials. But whatever we give, whether the dress is to be silk or calico, velvet or debege, it is always the latest style.

(Peterson's, June 1877)

Don't bring up the little girl to value people for what they have on; to centre [sic] all her little thoughts upon clothes; to make dress the staple of her conversation. . . . Don't be ashamed of untrimmed, turned, or neatly mended clothes; don't be ashamed of calico. You'll always look like a lady, if you cultivate the manners and scrupulous neatness of a true lady . . .

(The Complete Home, 1879)

Women of all station did their utmost to dress fashionably. The way a woman dressed had implications reaching far beyond her wish to appear attractive. Dress was considered the outer manifestation of an inner feminine essence. A woman negligent in her apparel was thought to be so in domestic affairs. A female careless of her appearance would as likely lack sweetness, propriety, and a love of order. While indicative of human character traits, costume was also prized for its facade. Victorians strove for the elegant and picturesque in their surroundings, and attractive costumes further beautified a setting. A woman's domain was largely confined to the home, where she was expected to be an adornment equal to its elegantly-appointed furniture and accessories. Outdoor amusements and sporting events, public entertainments and stately promenades were equally enhanced by charming ensembles. While women were not required to dress beyond their means and often admonished against squandering their

husband's earnings, becoming attire was nonetheless encouraged for its elevating effect upon the home and society, whether humble or exalted.

If dress revealed the personality, it also hinted at social standing. In the land of opportunity, people were constantly trying to climb the social ladder. Women forced by circumstance to work for their livelihood often let pride influence their pocketbook, using dress as a means to appear more prominent or respectable. Nor was this affectation limited to the working populace, as poor and middle classes alike spent an inordinate amount of time and money to clothe themselves according to the dictates of fashion. While the wealthy were far more able to afford the elaborate finery of the era, they too were affected by hard times or sudden financial reverses and shared equally in the desire to maintain appearances regardless of cost. Even women living on distant frontiers were not immune to the pressures of style, and fash-

ion magazines such as *Godey's Lady's Book* (1830), *Peterson's Ladies' National Magazine* (1842), and *Harper's Bazar* (1867) enabled them to keep abreast of the latest trends so they could dress appropriately as soon as circumstances allowed.

While not the only motive, the desire for stylish dress was a natural feminine instinct. Fetching garments heightened the charms of the wearer and allowed her to appear more pleasing to the opposite sex. Nor were gentlemen the only persons ladies tried to impress. Personal rivalry between friends and neighbors exhorted a strong influence. Everyone endeavored to dress as becomingly as their acquaintances, and the poor often emulated the rich to the detriment of their limited finances.

Fortunately, costly dress was not necessarily requisite. Most women aspired toward becoming a "lady," and fashion authorities were quick to clarify that the title was not synonymous with flashy or elaborate costume. A true lady did not wish to draw undue attention to herself. Her garments, like her manners, were simple and refined. Tasteful, well-fitted clothing cut in the latest style; clean fabric, cuffs, and collar; personal cleanliness and neatness; well-groomed hair—these marked a lady and were attainable to all income levels.

Fashion periodicals and other literature devoted much space to the importance of taste over money in matters like home decoration and dress and gave abundant suggestions for maintaining a pleasing appearance. Fashion plates showed not only the latest modes but more practical, yet stylish, everyday wear and frequently included the patterns necessary to duplicate them. By following their advice in purchasing less-expensive, though good-quality, fabrics; economizing in their usage; and either eliminating costly trim or keeping it to a minimum, women of lesser means were able to replicate fashionable outfits (which still needed the requisite corset, petticoats, etc., underneath). For those in especially straightened circumstances, a printed cotton material known as "calico" was a practical, though not necessarily welcome, option, for it was both affordable and durable—able to withstand frequent laundering and still look fresh and crisp. Such alternatives were feasible because it was neither fabric nor trim, but form and cut that insured a costume would be stylish in spite of its composition. Women were also advised to limit their amount of clothing and to purchase necessary articles like shoes and outer wraps late in the season, after prices had dropped.

Though clothing for the wealthier classes bore numerous labels, except for informal wear, the design remained virtually the same, varied by the richness of material, drapery, and trim. While differences might be slight, suitable attire was important and fluctuated with the occasion, requiring the fashionable woman to change clothing frequently. Her basic daytime attire consisted of a matinee jacket to wear while breakfasting or attending to her toilette; the morning wrapper for household duties; a plain, simple street dress for morning marketing; a house dress, skirt and blouse, or tea gown for afternoons spent quietly inside the home; stylish outfits for formal "visits" and promenades; and more elegant, often trained costumes for afternoon carriage rides. Sensible traveling clothes and gay "watering place" attire styled similarly to street clothes were periodically necessary for the resorts frequented by those escaping the summer heat. If the poor were not able to have the same quality, quantity, and variety of clothing as their wealthier counterparts, nor was it as necessary. Fancy negligée toilettes were less appropriate to humble abodes, carriage attire little required by women who had neither leisure time nor showy carriages, and traveling or watering place outfits useless to those who seldom ventured outside the confines of their town. Wrappers, simple home dresses, and stylish though plain outfits for the street nevertheless allowed them to present a neat, tidy, and up-to-date appearance. Fashion literature was also quick to reassure that to dress thus did not constitute stinginess but rather a commendable display of money-management and economy. Despite such assurances, however, many women put their families in debt to dress in a manner unsuited to their station.

From necessity, dresses were frequently altered as the years passed. Fashions changed rapidly as the fickle public (led by the Parisian autocrat Charles Worth) soon wearied of the familiar, and clothing alterations aided the quick dissemination of new styles to all levels of society. New trim and neckwear were sometimes sufficient to renovate the appearance. Faded clothes could be dyed in like or contrasting colors or ripped apart and "turned" inside out to expose the fresher side. Worn skirts might suffice for underskirts and lounge wear or have their useable surfaces fashioned into overskirts, plastrons, cuffs, button covers, and trim. Older garments could be remodeled to suit younger members of the household or used for afternoon costumes indoors. By following these and other money-saving ideas thoughtfully included in fashion magazines for "made overs," everyone was able to keep abreast of prevailing fashions.

Chapter Five

Evening Attire

Evening dress for ladies may be as rich, elegant and gay as one chooses to make it. . . . It may be cut either high or low at the neck, yet no lady should wear her dress so low as to make it quite noticeable or a special subject of remark.

(Our Deportment, 1882)

The richest velvets, the brightest and most delicate tints in silks, the most expensive laces, low neck and short sleeves, elaborate head-dress, the greatest display of gems, flowers, etc., all belong more or less to these occasions [the soiree and ball].

(Decorum, 1877)

The warm wrapper or dress is thrown aside; over the tightly drawn corsets is fastened a flimsy dress, with an inch of sleeve; the neck laid bare; thin stockings drawn on, in place of thick ones, and the consumption-seeker goes forth to the ball-room again.

(The Ladies' Book of Etiquette, 1873)

While it was considered improper to bare the upper arms or chest during daylight hours, these very same practices were encouraged for certain evening entertainments. Women were expected to dress appropriately depending on the occasion. Dresses for small dinner or social gatherings, while quite elegant, generally required more conservative necklines and long or elbow-length sleeves. If short sleeves or low necks were worn, they were accompanied by a lace or muslin covering. This policy eased by the 1880s, when any evening gown (referred to as "full dress") could feature short sleeves and a low neckline; the most elaborate ornamentation, however, was still reserved for gowns worn to operas or balls (which were usually given in private homes and distinguished from mere "dances" by the attendance of at least fifty guests). While etiquette writers warned that necklines should not be of a depth that would draw undo attention, these words were often ignored—especially among the more well endowed. Women were constantly warned about the dangers of cold—or worse, consumption—resulting from their scanty evening attire.

Except for sleeves and necklines, evening styles were similar in form to their daytime contemporaries. Some differences did exist, as gowns generally fastened at the back, where they were often laced rather than hooked or buttoned; sometimes contained overskirts when these were not in fashion for day wear; and were made from costlier, more ornately-trimmed fabrics. The two-piece skirt and bodice predominated. Bodices were in greatest demand, their expense compensated in part when matched with simpler skirts from other ensembles. Eighteen-sixties ball dresses featured short puffed sleeves and off-the-shoulder necklines, either straight or with a slight dip at the center front, which became more rounded or squared as the decade progressed.

In addition to these styles, square-neck sleeveless gowns became fashionable by the mid-seventies and would remain so throughout the eighties, when a bow or rosette often embellished the shoulder. Also in vogue by the eighties were round, wide V, or heart-shaped necklines, worn with off- or just off-the-shoulder straps, either sleeveless or with close-fitting, demi-sleeves. While necklines saw little change, the nineties no longer favored fully-bared shoulders, and sleeves became a prominent feature. Gowns of the first few years could have small puff sleeves; thin shoulder straps separating off-the-shoulder sleeves (which left the upper portion of the shoulder and arm exposed); or be sleeveless, with the still-popular bows featured at the top. By the mid-nineties most sleeves had become enormous balloons, some extending almost to the elbow, and bodices were embellished with the exaggerated berthas, revers, and epaulets popular on day wear. Toward the end of the decade the smaller "puffs" returned, and some gowns even possessed long, wrist-length sleeves. Trains were standard on evening wear from the late sixties through the early eighties, and were commonly featured, but not an absolute necessity, after that time.

The bare arms and necks featured in most styles provided a perfect showplace for necklaces and bracelets. Diamonds, considered vulgar when displayed during the day, were encouraged for more formal evening entertainments. While lower arms were exposed when dining, perfect-fitting gloves (generally above-the-elbow) reappeared at the end of the meal, garnished by fancy bracelets. Fans were almost universally clasped within, relaying unspoken messages to gentlemen by the way they were held. Though hairstyles differed little from daytime, hair was lavishly embellished—especially for balls and operas—with ribbons, beads, feathers, and real or artificial flowers (which were also used to adorn gowns).

Simple, early-sixties evening gown: back-lacing bodice with straight, off-the-shoulders neckline ornamented by flower corsage; short, wide sleeves. Washington, D.C.

Early-sixties printed gown with low, straight, off-the-shoulder neckline partially covered by shawl; wide, elbow-length pagoda sleeves. Jewelry consists of matching bracelets, big oval brooch, and large beaded choker with cameo center. Cincinnati, Ohio.

Sixties, off-the-shoulder gown dips slightly mid-center; wide short sleeves; matching bracelets (possibly diamonds). Flowers ornament long ringlets. Reading, Pennsylvania.

Mid-sixties, off-the-shoulder gown accompanied by long, elegant lace shawl. Large beaded necklace with cross. NM TS (since removed)

Mid-sixties, elaborate, off-the-shoulder gown. Lavish jewels (diamonds?) garnish neck, ears, and wrists. New York, New York. TS (Possibly celebrity)

Elegant, mid- to late-sixties fringed, off-the-shoulder gown. Flower-strewn sausage curls. New York, New York.

Seventies sleeveless gown with rounded neckline heavily embellished with what appears to be flowers. Wide black ribbon choker with large locket. Feather in hair. NM

Low, off-the-shoulder neckline of seventies gown reveals some cleavage. Thick necklace with locket. New York, New York.

HOWELL,   867 & 869 B'WAY.

Exquisite sixties embossed, off-the-shoulder evening gown with overskirt. Flowers embellish both hair and bodice. New York, New York (Possibly celebrity)

Conservative (possibly dinner) dress, bustled and trained with long overskirt. High-necked, front-buttoning, short-sleeved cuirass bodice. Matching bangle bracelets. c. 1875-76. Evanston, Illinois.

Early-seventies gown with low, rounded decolletage and short sleeves. Necklace; wide matching bracelets; dangling earrings. Bridgeport, Connecticut.

Elegant sleeveless, mid-seventies bustled and trained gown heavily strewn with flowers. Simple black choker at neck. New York, New York. (Possibly celebrity)

PURCHASED FROM
CHARLES L. RITZMANN.
"CELEBRITIES"

228 FIFTH AVENUE.
NEAR 27TH ST.
NEW YORK

Sleeveless, off-the-shoulder gown, partially covered by shawl, reveals some cleavage. Black choker with locket overlaid by long, beaded necklace. Dangling cameo earrings. Fancy comb and flowers in hair. Brooklyn, New York. (Possibly celebrity)

Fredricks   Brooklyn N. Y.

Short, demi-sleeved, late-seventies evening dress. Long, dangling earrings; pearl necklace. San Francisco, California. (Celebrity)

Ellie Wilton.

BRADLEY & RULOFSON, SAN FRANCISCO

Late-seventies short, demi-sleeved gown features conservative, lace-embellished V neck. Dangling earrings; thick necklace with center extension. Boston, Massachusetts.

Late-seventies/early-eighties square-neck sleeveless gown. Cleavage hidden by large locket, which depends from center suspension of thick linked necklace. San Francisco, California. (Celebrity)

ADELINA PATTI.   Copyright, 1882, by J. M. Mora.

Mora   707 BROADWAY, N.Y.

Elegant, early-eighties conservative (probably dinner) gown with square neckline, elbow-length sleeves, and long gloves. New York, New York. (Celebrity) Card imprinted "1882."

Mid-eighties
sleeveless, V neck
gown embellished
with row of flowers.
Long, deeply-
pointed bodice laces
in back; apron-shape
overskirt surmounts
pleated underskirt.
Long gloves reach
almost to shoulders.
Chicago, Illinois.
(Possibly celebrity)

High, square neckline and huge sleeves divided by black velvet tabs distinguish elegant, mid-nineties evening gown. Hair has prominent top knot. Huntsville, Missouri.

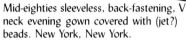

Mid-eighties sleeveless, back-fastening, V neck evening gown covered with (jet?) beads. New York, New York.

Mid-eighties sleeveless gown with shallow, rounded, lace-embellished neckline. NM

Mid-nineties evening dress with conservative, rounded neckline surrounded by deep lace, large puffed sleeves, and lace-framed plastron. Simple choker appears to have tiny padlocks. Charleston, South Carolina.

Simple, mid-nineties gown with high, rounded neckline; large balloon sleeves topped by deep lace epaulets; loose fabric center front of corsage. Greenfield, Massachusetts.

BLANCHE L. BATES.

Low square neckline with thin straps divided from full, off-the-shoulder sleeves leaves upper shoulders bare. Ornamental, triangular-shaped plastron. c. 1895. San Francisco, California. (Celebrity)

Mid-nineties, long-sleeved gown with huge balloon sleeves and high, squared neckline. Sacramento, California.

Chapter Six

Clothing Manufacture

There is another evil demanding our earnest consideration, and it is one of the growing evils of the day. I mean the immense labor bestowed on all the garments, and extending to every article that is worn, so that those whose circumstances demand economy must give a large portion of their time to the making and embellishing of their wardrobes.

(Dress Reform, 1874)

Many ladies remember the slow and tedious process of Dress-Cutting which was in general use ten years ago [before the availability of dress patterns], and the distressing doubt and uncertainty which was always felt lest the material, beautiful and costly as it often was, should be rendered nearly valueless by a bad or inaccurate fit. No rules existing except the Dress-makers own judgment, uniformity of excellence could not be expected. One good fit was no guarantee for the next; every new dress requiring the same long wearisome process of pinning and cutting to fit the form, trying and retrying before it finally reaches the hands of the owner.

(Godey's, October 1862)

To make a Frock.—The best way for a novice is to get a dress fitted (not sewed) at the best mantua-maker's. Then take out a sleeve, rip it to pieces, and cut out a paper pattern. Then take out half of the waist . . . and cut out a pattern . . . When this is done, a lady of common ingenuity can cut and fit a dress by these patterns.

(American Woman's Home, 1869)

By mid-nineteenth century manufactured fabrics largely replaced homespun, and clothing previously constructed tediously by hand began to be sewn with the aid of Elias Howe's recently-patented (1846) lockstitch sewing machine. Large firms were the first to use the costly, hand- or foot-powered device to manufacture difficult garments such as men's wear and ladies' hoops, corsets, and outer wraps, which were the first items available "ready-made." Independent dressmakers purchased machines as soon as finances would allow, their cost-effectiveness assured by the completion of many more garments within the same time frame. By the end of the Civil War, mass production enabled the sewing machine to become an affordable commodity for most middle and upper class families. While unquestionably easing the work involved in sewing, fashion seemed to compensate for this advantage by increasing trim and other elaboration upon garments. As a result, most women continued to spend a great deal of their time fabricating the vast plethora of garments dictated essential by the tyranny of fashion.

To help lessen the burden of the housewife in supplying the enormous clothing demands of large Victorian families, upper and middle class households often hired a seamstress. For several days or weeks during the spring and fall, she would either work out of her own dwelling or reside with the family to help produce clothing sufficient

for the coming hot or cold weather. Sometimes seamstresses executed the difficult planning and cutting of the garment to insure an accurate fit, with the actual sewing, or at least the machine-applied trim and hand-finish work, completed by the customer. Often, the seamstress made the more precise-fitting bodices (or these could later be purchased ready-made) while the client constructed the less-fitted skirts. When in vogue, the inexperienced sewer might even welcome overskirts (if not too elaborately draped), as they hid any defects in the skirt below.

While stricter finances assured the lower classes would have to make their own garments, sewing machines lessened the burden for families who followed the advice of fashion magazines and pooled their resources for its purchase, then took turns using the device (or borrowed one from a more fortunate neighbor). By the turn of the century, the cost would so diminish that the labor-saving tool would be within reach of almost everyone.

Before the arrival of clothing patterns, women visited experienced dressmakers to have their garments custom fit. After a long and tiring process of shaping the fabric to the individual and countless adjustments and refitting, an outfit was eventually fashioned. If necessary, the homemaker could then tear it apart to trace patterns for constructing additional garments—at least until clothing styles changed. By mid-century other options began to emerge. Pattern diagrams slowly appeared in fashion magazines, though these needed to be traced onto other paper and enlarged. The enterprising Ellen Demorest began experimenting with full-size tissue paper patterns, including one as a premium in each issue of *Madame Demorest's Mirror of Fashions*, which debuted in 1860. While an improvement, both methods had to be adjusted for size. Mail-order companies charged a fee in exchange for patterns custom-made to fit the customer's individual measurements. Often, disassembling one's own costumes for guides remained easier and cheaper. This began to change after 1863, when Ebenezer Butterick patented his creation of tissue paper patterns in standardized sizes for boys' clothing. By 1866, the line extended to include patterns for women's wrappers, with street wear soon to follow. (Fashion magazines would continue to supply their less exacting "free" patterns, which often needed to be separated from a confusing maze of overlaid diagrams.) With much of the time and guess work removed from planning the garment, more stylish and precise-fitting clothing was accessible to everyone (and at considerable savings, since there was less need for a dressmaker's services).

By the 1870s, large department stores were beginning to emerge in the major cities, and mail order was becoming a growing industry. While supplying countless household necessities and men's wear, clothing for women was still limited to outdoor wraps; undergarments such as corsets, bustles, drawers, chemises, petticoats, and stockings; the simple household wrapper; and a few items of street dress. This inventory would expand by the early-eighties to include a large assortment of women's daytime apparel, but since sewing one's own clothing was more cost-effective, and the rich preferred more elegant, custom-made garments, fabrics enjoyed far wider sales than ready-made clothing. The sewing machine and precision patterns allowed many women to construct their own and much of their families' everyday clothing, perhaps reserving some of their hard-earned funds to hire a seamstress for the more intricate or tedious articles or purchasing them ready made. As in all periods when finances allowed, ladies might frequent the finer dressmaking establishments located in the larger cities. Those possessing wealth sufficient for European travel could have their wardrobes created by the most exclusive Paris modistes. Even the wealthy were cautioned to be proficient in sewing, however, so they could instruct their children and oversee the work of others, as well as safeguard against possible reversals of their own fortunes.

Chapter Seven

Laundry

If possible, have only one washing-day in a week; have one every week, for if clothes lie long soiled they are harder to wash, and wear out faster. Have, if possible, the washing day early in the week. Remember that washing is very hard work; more young women break down their strength with washing than with any other toil: therefore, go at it reasonably.

(The Complete Home, 1879)

It is very important that the clothing should be kept clean. That which is worn for a long time becomes saturated with the excretions and exhalations of the body, which prevent free transpiration from the pores of the skin, and thereby induce mental inactivity and depression of the physical powers. Unclean clothing may be the means of conveying disease . . .

(The People's Common Sense Medical Adviser, Revised Edition, 1895)

The really dainty woman takes thought for every item of her apparel . . . On taking off a gown, she does not hang or lay it away until it has been properly aired, cleansed and repaired.

(Delineator, April 1895)

Even the simplest, most conservative Victorian dress was constructed from a considerable amount of material, and most clothing was lined and laden in varying degrees with lace, ruffles, fringe, or other decoration. Plain or fancy, it required cleaning—the most difficult and detested chore among all women's duties. If domestic servants were employed, the task often fell to them. Otherwise, a laundress might be hired to come to the home or attend to the clothing at her own residence. Even persons of modest means managed to set aside funds for this luxury. Those not so fortunate usually chose Monday for washing, as many articles were changed on Sunday and stains would not be given sufficient time to set. Wrinkled clothes were promptly ironed the following day.

While the poor might be forced to wash their clothing outdoors in large tubs over an open flame, most families utilized the stationary basins, copper boilers, and stoves located in their kitchen or its adjacent laundry room, or in the basement. Fabrics were initially sorted into whites and delicates, colored articles, and woolens. White undergarments, shirts, collars, cuffs, and other clothing—along with bedding and table linens—were washed first. A large receptacle received one portion at a time, which was immersed in water that flowed directly from the tap or, in unplumbed residences, entailed more laborious retrieval from a pump or well. Homes lacking primitive water heating systems required the less-timely services of a stove or the increasingly-outmoded fireplace to produce a temperature just bearable to sensitive hands. Before soap could be added to the heated mixture, shavings from the large bars needed to be dissolved into boiling water. All but the most delicate articles were then thoroughly scrubbed. Though a washboard generally sufficed, wealthier families might avail themselves of the hand-agitated washing machines attainable for home use after the Civil War. (While meant to alleviate part of the washday burden, these primitive, small-capacity machines often caused additional problems, for they were prone to leaking and tended to tear clothing or leave them stained from rusting bolts.) Harsher chemicals like sal soda or lye might be added with moderation to help loosen dirt but were not meant to replace scrubbing. After washing, clothes were placed in a clean receptacle where they were boiled for thirty minutes, the self-agitation forcing hot soapy water throughout the fabric, effectively disbursing any remaining dirt and disease-breeding microbes. From there they were transferred for rinsing, with bluing added to prevent yellowing. These were the minimum requirements—stricter housewives required pre-soaking and additional scrubbing and rinsing.

Once clean, clothes were painstakingly wrung by hand or forced through a hand-cranked wringer to free them from excess water. Those articles requiring firmness were dipped in homemade starch, which had been mixed, cooked, and strained beforehand, and wrung again. After being turned inside-out, garments were dried upon indoor drying racks or outside clothes lines (with the latter method preferred, as fresh air and sunlight purportedly sweetened and whitened clothing).

Silks and woolens required more careful laundering. Surface cleansing by sponging with a mixture of ammonia and water was generally considered safest. If woolens were immersed, a quick, gentle rubbing in warm water sufficed, and slight squeezing replaced wringing, which could leave material wrinkled and puckered. Colored articles too were denied the boiling that could shrink or fade fabrics and were aided by a handful of salt in the rinse to prevent bleeding. As harsh sunlight might cause further discoloration, they were either dried indoors or placed expressly in the shade. Whether thick wool or light cotton, all fabrics became heavier when wet, and stooping and reaching to hang them to dry—not to mention the scrubbing, wringing, and lugging required beforehand—taxed all the energies of the poor housewife or laundress on "blue" Monday.

The equally difficult task of ironing monopolized the following day. To make creases more amenable, clothing was sprinkled by hand or with a wetted whisk broom and rolled in towels to maintain dampness. A hot fire kept several irons ready for use, and both outer- and underclothing required pressing from cast irons that could weigh from four to ten pounds. In addition, collars, cuffs, and trim often enlisted the special services of fluting, crimping, or ruffling irons. Heat was difficult to regulate, and frequent applications of beeswax to the bottom of the implement were necessary to keep it moving smoothly across the fabric. Upon completion, irons and all other washday apparatus received a thorough scrubbing to prevent the lingering odor of stale soap suds and render them clean for their next usage. Before

clothing could be put away, any bodice boning or temporary stitching (generally used to mold overskirt drapery) that had been removed to facilitate laundering and ironing needed to be reinserted and re-stitched!

All garments required attending after wear to lengthen the time between washing. Upon removal clothing was placed upon a chair or other furniture for airing to eliminate dampness and perspiration odor. After the garment was sufficiently dry, beating, shaking, and brushing effectively disbursed most mud and dust particles that might still be clinging to the fabric. Apparel was next examined for stains, their cause determining which of the many spot-removing receipts would effect the best treatment. Any tears were quickly repaired so additional wear or the vigorous process of washing would not inflict further damage. Outfits were then hung on closet hooks or neatly folded in drawers until worn sufficiently to warrant overall cleaning. With proper care, clothes made from durable fabrics could last an entire season without laundering. (This was a worthwhile effort since all washing was difficult, and it was even recommended that the popular heavy woolen dresses be ripped apart for easier management during the washing and ironing process and then reconstructed!)

Chapter Eight

Personal Hygiene

Many people may be met with whose skins have never known the sensation of water, excepting the parts visible to the eye. Hundreds and thousands have never had a bath, and a still greater number only as an exceptional case, when ordered as a part of some plan of medical treatment. Yet it is well known that health depends upon a frequent ablution of the whole body; and, though a bath is the most convenient and complete method of carrying out the process, yet, by means of a sponge or any similar object, it may be effected sufficiently to cleanse the pores.

(Godey's, February 1862)

It is, indeed, incredible, when we consider the importance of the exhalation performed by the skin, to what extent ablution is neglected, not only . . . in charitable institutions and seminaries for the young, but by ladies, in ordinary circumstances, to whom the use of the bath could be productive of no inconvenience.

(The Ladies' Book of Etiquette, 1873)

[Women] have, perhaps, been taught, as many have, to look upon water with a certain amount of distrust, and consider the daily washing of the face, hands and neck, and a general ablution, once a week, quite sufficient for reasonable cleanliness.

(Demorist's, April 1876)

In most of our houses in the city there is a separate bath room with hot and cold water, but country houses are not always so arranged. A substitute for the bath-room is a large piece of oilcloth, which can be laid upon the floor of the ordinary dressing-room. Upon this may be placed the bath-tub or basin.

(Decorum, 1877)

While dusty, unpaved streets were largely accountable for soiling the surface of clothing, lack of personal hygiene could be even more detrimental. Indoor bathing facilities were not that uncommon during the mid- to late-Victorian period—it was more a matter of whether one had the means, inclination, or sufficient water supply to take advantage of them. Indoor "bath rooms" and "water closets" were often featured in mid-century architectural books for the grand homes of the wealthy, sometimes including shower heads over tubs and fixed sinks in bedrooms. Bathrooms were included in the renderings of many middle class homes during the seventies, where they would be commonly pictured by the eighties. (Unfortunately, most homes constructed before then remained without this luxury.) Improvements in plumbing and the growth of public sewers and water works during the first two decades of the twentieth century made indoor plumbing for even the poorer city dweller both more

Footed, metal portable shower set up in bedroom. The lady inside is screened by checkered fabric. The woman in her petticoats gets ready to pull a cord, releasing the flow of water overhead. (A hand pump located at the base of the shower refills upper reservoir.) Stereo card simply titled "The Shower Bath." c. 1860s.

desirable and obtainable. Country inhabitants lacking such public facilities continued to supply their own plumbing systems, if so desired (a necessity in some areas throughout the twentieth century).

City residents had the option of purchasing water from public water works, where available. Otherwise, it was feasible to obtain indoor running water for both city and country homes through gravitational flow from a large wood or metal cistern, which was situated preferably in the attic, as water stored in outside tanks could freeze in the wintertime. Attic reservoirs were popularly filled with rainwater that had accumulated on the roof—with any excess often guided by gutters to special underground cisterns, where it was filtered and stored. Wells might be dug in areas with insufficient rainfall, and the water from these, along with that in underground cisterns, then needed conveying up to the attic. While windmills were effective, from an aesthetic viewpoint, force pumps were preferred, as they could be hidden within the cellar where they were regularly (and frequently daily) worked by the servants employed in upper and middle class homes. Water could also be obtained from a nearby spring and transmitted to the house through the aid of gravity flow or a hydraulic ram (if at a lower elevation). Inhabitants of unplumbed residents (either from necessity or personal preference) continued to retrieve their water in pails from outdoor streams, wells, pumps, or urban hydrants to supply the needs of clothes and dish washing, drinking, cooking, and bathing.

Despite its convenience, running water was expensive and not necessarily a desirable inclusion in the home. The labor involved in hand pumping; the inadequacy of plumbing, which often stopped up or froze in the winter; the danger of explosion from boilers used to heat water or from drinking water contaminated by lead pipes; the foul smelling "sewer gasses," which emanated from bathroom fixtures and were said to cause disease; and the removal of household waste into often improperly-constructed "cesspools," which needed periodic cleansing and whose contents often leached into the soil, further contaminating drinking water, all made indoor plumbing a less-welcome commodity than one may have supposed for the nineteenth-century homeowner.

Many households considered it unhygienic to bring the common privy indoors. This was partly due to the sewer gasses (literally, air spoiled by human waste) emanating therein, which were responsible for the placement of bathing facilities and water closets in separate rooms. Though this practice waned by the 1870s, fear of prolonged contact lingered, especially during sleeping hours when the body was believed more susceptible to blood poisoning. Some homes contained only bathing facilities; others had water closets positioned against an outside wall, preferably in the servant's wing. There they could receive window ventilation at a safe distance from family bed chambers (and also be situated conveniently above kitchen plumbing). Architectural books contained instructions for constructing a water trap, which consisted of a U-shaped bend in the pipe where water lay. This, combined with vent piping, effectively blocked toxic odors from re-entering the house. These guidelines were either insufficient or ignored, however, as the problem persisted throughout the era.

Even if one did not enjoy the convenience of indoor plumbing, a pitcher and wash basin was accessible to everyone. A brisk cold-water sponging two to three times a week, adding soap if performed less frequently, was at first considered sufficient. By the seventies, most authorities advised a thorough cleansing by a hip- or sponge bath every morning (using an oil cloth to protect the bedroom floor), with a full warm bath in a portable tub indulged in once a week. Even in homes with plumbing, few possessed more than one bathroom. As families were large and the daily water supply generally limited to the attic tank, portable or stationery bedroom wash basins probably endured the greatest use. While portable basins could only be furnished with warm water if it was painstakingly heated on the kitchen stove and hauled upstairs, hot water was an available luxury in houses with plumbing. There it could be heated either by a gas boiler situated next to the tub or a copper boiler attached to the kitchen range (which received cold water by gravity flow from upstairs, forcing the newly heated water back up into the chamber). While cold baths (along with showers) were promoted as invigorating and hot as sedative, the majority regarded the tepid bath safest for the nervous system and overall health.

By 1860, both physicians and the writers of etiquette books strongly advocated personal cleanliness. Physicians believed that clean pores prevented many diseases by enabling the skin to breathe in oxygen and expel excess body wastes and carbonic acid. Etiquette writers felt it the duty of every decent, well-bred person, male or female, to appear clean, tidy, and inoffensive. Many people, regardless of station, did not heed this advice. After all, advocates for cleanliness did not even arise until mid-century. Before that time most people bathed only once or twice a year, believing the body's natural oils kept their skin supple and protected them from disease. Only when the public became accustomed to using various "water cures" for medicinal purposes did they realize bathing could be beneficial. In time, gentlemen would frequent such varieties as the Russian or Turkish steam baths for their cleansing as well as restorative properties (related to the "sweating-out" of colds, fever, ague, and malarial diseases); women might patronize them in preparation for a ball or other evening entertainment. Old habits were hard to change, however, and writers throughout the sixties and seventies were appalled at the want of cleanliness—even among proper ladies—remarking that many bathed only their face, neck, and hands with any regularity. Indeed it was not uncommon to encounter people who, though particular about their persons, would go for weeks or even months without benefit of a bath. While many continued regularly cleansing only their visible extremities during the eighties, more were taking advantage of the sponge bath. This trend continued to grow during the nineties, though a quick spattering of cool water in a room often of like temperature was largely ineffectual. Widespread improvements in physical hygiene would await the new century, when reliable water heating systems and an unlimited supply of public water became more available.

Proper care of the teeth was considered as important as a clean body, though these too were often sadly neglected by the general populace. Those inclined to read about the subject were advised to brush morning and night, using water alone or in combination with various tooth powder preparations. They were also urged to visit a dentist, who could remove accumulated tartar and fill cavities. If tooth decay was too far advanced, teeth were pulled and a false set fashioned. While bad breath was an acknowledged concern and mouthwashes containing chloride of lime or the chewing of common parsley might be recommended, it was generally agreed that proper care of the teeth and digestive system would eliminate the problem.

Though hair received much consideration, the methods elicited to keep it clean and shiny were woefully inadequate. Too much reliance fell solely upon brushing. Fifteen minutes morning and evening was deemed adequate to remove the day's dust and keep the skin clean, as well as stimulate circulation, distribute oils, and promote luster. While some authorities recommended washing the hair once a week, most believed once or twice a month sufficient. Many feared more frequent scrubbing would remove necessary oils (especially as many soaps contained harsh substances such as alkaline lyes), leaving hair dull and brittle. For those whose locks were dry or had a tendency to scurf, hair oils or pomades made from unsavory substances such as salad oil, bear's grease, or beef marrow were applied to the scalp (though moderation was stressed in their usage). These were intended to supplement natural oil glands to help strengthen hair, prevent dryness, and promote growth. This application of greasy ointments, combined with the lack of cleansing, inevitably resulted in many scalps laden with grease, dust, and perspiration.

Chapter Nine

Cosmetics

So universal has this custom of "painting" become in this enlightened and advanced age of ours, that no lady's toilet is considered complete unless the face be bedaubed with a coat of whitewash, and the lips, cheeks, and eyebrows painted and pencilled up . . . to meet views of foolish ideas of beauty. Ladies high, low, rich, and poor indulge in the deleterious practice, and the quantities of lily white, lemon rouge, chalk, starch, flour, carmine, and Indian ink, they annually rub into their skin, makes us wonder how nature withstands the abuse as long as she does.

(Godey's, January, 1869)

We cannot but allude to the practice of using paints, a habit strongly to be condemned. If for no other reason than that poison lurks beneath every layer, inducing paralytic affections and premature death, they should be discarded—but they are a disguise which deceives no one, even at a distance; there is a ghastly deathliness in the appearance of the skin after it has been painted, which is far removed from the natural hue of health.

(Decorum, 1877)

And, after dressing for the evening, look again at your reflection in the mirror, and study the effect. Do you resemble a painted doll or an elegant woman? Is the expression killed by cosmetics or improved?

(Gems of Deportment, 1881)

A clean body and mouth, combined with soft skin, shiny hair, and sometimes even a little artificial help to enhance one's natural beauty, completed the picture of the well-groomed, tastefully-attired person. Etiquette books from the 1870s onward recommended numerous preparations for skin care. Vaseline or cold creams compounded from almond oil, white wax, and spermaceti helped soften skin. Assorted concoctions controlled skin eruptions—though cleanliness was believed the best guard against blemishes. While parasols abounded to protect ladies delicate faces from the sun, numerous potions incorporating lemon juice faded tans or freckles in the case of accidental sunburn. To control perspiration odor, some writers suggested mixing compound spirits of ammonia, tincture of benzoin, or aromatic herbs with the bath water. As this undoubtedly proved ineffectual for many, cologne could also be made at home—with light scents preferred, as heavier fragrances were viewed an effort to mask unpleasant odors.

Not only theatrical artists but women of all walks had the option of using an amazing variety of artifice to enhance their natural charms. Victorian writers accepted these efforts in varying degrees. The use of a lip salve containing red dye was one of the few admissible practices. Face powder produced from starch was intended for light application so it would not lie "caked" upon facial crevasses, with one containing a rosy tint preferred to the separate application of rouge. If acne or other blemishes marred the skin, liquid cover-ups were available, also

with the caution that they be applied sparingly. Imperfections such as warts could be removed with the aid of a caustic stick, with surgical application suggested for unsightly moles. Dark, brilliant eyes were so coveted that some women risked their sight by applying poisonous belladonna to dilate the pupils and add false luster. Surrounding eyelashes were encouraged to grow long by periodic trimming and could be darkened by the application of elderberry juice, burnt cork, or India ink. Dyeing the eye lids was felt to be vulgar as well as dangerous, however, and moderation was stressed when penciling the brows to preserve the natural harmony of nature's tints.

Hair, the acknowledged crowning glory of both men and women, also occasioned considerable notice. Superfluous body hair could be plucked or removed with the aid of depilatories. Applications of egg white, beeswax, or isinglass stiffened hair to maintain the shapes created from hair pins and papers or curling irons. Bleached hair was considered detestable, and hair dyes were often condemned for being made from poisonous substances—with the exception of the natural product obtained from the hull of black walnuts. Dandruff was an indicator of the low bred, and the oil and pomade remedies were similar to those recommended for dry hair. The use of false hair to supplement one's own tresses was a semi-accepted practice promoted in fashion magazines throughout the period. False bangs or shallow front pieces were often a welcome addition necessary to cover areas thinned by the excessive use of hot curling irons. Pre-formed switches and buns greatly lessened the time needed to fashion intricate hairstyles—though so great were the quantities sometimes required to be fashionable that women complained of the added weight or of the heat generated beneath. Long tresses were standard for adult women; however, cutting hair short following fevers or severe illness allegedly induced a fresh, silken growth.

Though nature could be supplemented in any number of ways, the general consensus was that all artifice should be avoided—with proper diet, bathing, and exercise believed sufficient to eliminate most problems. If cosmetics or hair products were used, their application should defy detection.

Part II

Ladies' Daytime Street Apparel

Transition Periods

American styles were dictated by Paris, the city where fashions were not only conceived (predominantly by the brilliant Charles Worth from the famed House of Worth) but manifested into the fashion illustrations so critical in disseminating the latest trends to the rest of the world. Developments originating on the continent could take a year or more before materializing upon the American public. French plates once received across the ocean needed to be re-engraved and reprinted into local periodicals. Often they were modified and then redrawn to ensure acceptance by the more practical-minded American audience. (French plates characteristically depicted elaborate costumes worn, at best, by only the highest strata of society—Americans as a whole preferring styles less opulent than their European counterparts.)

Once introduced to the states, fashions were not necessarily accepted overnight. The wealthy or more fashion conscious might quickly adopt innovative styles, while other, perhaps less-affluent women, clung from necessity to their more outmoded costumes. Fashion trends were also communicated to those living in larger cities more quickly than outlying areas. Sometimes outfits incorporated lingering traits of a previous period with newer innovations just introduced, or older outfits were remodeled to resemble those currently in vogue. Hairstyles too could fall into this category, though for different reasons. Women sporting the most up-to-date fashions might find what they considered a flattering hairstyle hard to relinquish; conversely, women who could not afford new dresses could, with very little effort and no capital outlay, feel more fashionable by changing their hair. Most young and middle-aged women did their utmost to be in vogue despite personal circumstances. Older women more set in their ways, however, often preferred the familiar to "newfangled" styles, and it was not uncommon to see them wearing hairstyles or clothing several years out of date.

A lady's conduct is never so entirely at the mercy of critics, because never so public, as when she is in the street. Her dress, carriage, walk, will all be exposed to notice; every passer-by will look at her, if it is only for one glance; every unladylike action will be marked; and in no position will a dignified, ladylike deportment be more certain to command respect.

Let me start with you upon your promenade, my friend, and I will soon decide your place upon the list of well-bred ladies.

First, your dress . . .

(The Ladies' Book of Etiquette, 1873)

Chapter Ten

1860-1864

An air of elegance and refinement exuded from restrained outfits and subdued hairstyles. Clothing was prim and proper, lacking drapery, displaying little ornamentation, and leaving no skin visible beneath the neck other than the hands. The only ostentation consisted in the vast quantities of often-elegant fabric needed to construct the voluminous skirts. Emphasis was placed on contrasting the upper and lower torso with the central, tiny waist; wide skirts, full sleeves, and horizontal trim all served toward this purpose.

Outfits

Outfits consisted of a skirt and waist-length bodice that were constructed separately and then frequently sewn together at the waistband to prevent gaps along the mid-section. The matching ensemble was generally formed from solid-colored fabrics, though checks, polka dots, stripes, and small prints enjoyed significant favor. The skirt possessed a side-front opening, or "placket," with its waistband concealed by a bodice that fastened down the center front using buttons or hidden hooks and eyes. Sometimes buttons were merely ornamental, the bodice fastening invisibly underneath, and on rare occasions diagonal placements were seen.

Most bodices (or "corsages") fit snug against the body using vertical darts along the waist, as bust line darts were not employed during the Victorian period. To give fabric a smooth appearance and help maintain its shape, bodices were "boned" by inserting several narrow strips of whalebone along the seams and darts within the front and sides of the lining. The corsage ended precisely at the natural waist, often forming double points that extended in varying depths upon the front of the skirt (with single points generally reserved for evening wear or the back of the dress). Occasionally bodice material was gathered into a waistband, producing a fuller, less constricted look. This created only an illusion of comfort, however, as most proved to be mere shells over form-fitting underbodices—which attached along the side, shoulder, and waist seams and were often boned. Further boning appeared in the corsets worn underneath to help slim the figure and smooth unsightly bulges. These did not need to be exceedingly tight, as wide skirts and sleeves helped give the appearance of a tiny waist without requiring heavy cinching.

Although applied sparingly, trim embellished an occasional bodice. It might materialize horizontally across the bosom, possibly extending upon the arm; as a line down the center closure; or defining the "points" at the hem. Often the only ornament interrupting the surface consisted of the small buttons used to close the corsage or a narrow fabric belt, which was frequently worn over bodices of a "rounded," or uniform, depth at the hem. Both were often distinguished by contrasting colors. Belts could be plain, fastening invisibly with hooks and eyes, or enhanced with a large rectangular or oval-shaped buckle. On rare occasions a "Swiss" belt (or cummerbund) was substituted, which widened at the center to form points above and below the waist.

Shirts offered a fashionable alternative to the bodice. Though considered suitable street attire only for young women, they were permissible to a wider age range for casual wear inside the home. As fabrics did not have to match, shirts were often promoted in fashion literature as an economical means of utilizing skirts whose bodices, which suffered more wear and tear, had since worn-out. The popular "Garibaldi" was frequently colored and had distinctive narrow trim where it fastened down the center front and along

Group of females, all wearing full bodices gathered into waistband. Saratoga Springs, New York. TS

the top of the shoulder, cuffs, and waistband. Shirt fabric did not extend below the waist but was sewn in gathers to a separate waistband, which could fit over that of the skirt, displaying its decorative trim, or be hidden beneath a belt. Fashion magazines sometimes featured close-fitting jackets that fastened at the center, leaving the chest and midriff exposed. These were worn over separate undersleeves and a long sleeveless, side-less "chemisette" (perhaps accompanied by a vest), which were cleverly contrived to give the appearance of a shirt. Far more common, though, was the standard white "Spencer" or "waist." These plain shirts were generally concealed in part by a shawl, "corslet," or open jacket. Resembling a large Swiss belt, the corslet reached under the bosom, sometimes continuing into dropped shoulder straps.

The popular, hip-length "Zouave" jacket featured wide, full sleeves. Collarless, it fastened at the throat and then curved outward to expose the shirt underneath. (A similar look was often simulated by trim applied to the ordinary bodice.)

Older women throughout the Victorian period often clung to the outmoded styles of a few years past, and many now preferred a corsage whose popularity had waned by the late fifties. Known as the "fan-shaped bodice," it was constructed with pleats or gathers at the center front, the material radiating from there to the shoulders in the shape of a fan. The neckline could either be enclosed or form a wide-open V, which was properly filled by a chemisette (lesser known as a "vestee" or "habit shirt") firmly anchored about the waist with ties.

Skirts were notable for their great volume, which effectively hid the figure from the waist down (though the sway of the hoop exposed an occasional ankle). They were

Lots of trim: skirt bottom, bodice points, and interesting overlay design on sleeve. NM TS

generally formed from straight lengths of material or from fabric gored (or narrowed) minimally toward the waist. Pleats neatly directed toward the center of the dress effectively reduced the great quantities of fabric around the waistline. Also achieving the desired fullness at the hips, they encouraged fabric to fall outward in soft folds. Large utilitarian pockets were included at the sides, invisibly accessed through vertical slits hidden along the seams.

Skirts were initially of uniform fullness and depth, which could vary anywhere from floor length to several inches removed. By the last year of the period the emphasis began to shift toward the rear, where they expanded outward (with the hoops beneath following suit) and had a tendency to just brush upon the floor. Narrow hem protectors fashioned from braided fabric lined the bottom to protect it from fraying or excessive soiling, and the "porte jupe" or "dress elevator" quickly materialized as a further safeguard. This inventive device loosely resembled a modern day garter belt. Resting directly below the dress, it contained eight long cords that, when attached near the hem and pulled taught at the waist (where they met after being threaded through a clever arrangement of casings), effectively lifted costly fabrics above street level. Another, more simple apparatus, which could be constructed inexpensively at home, fit outside the dress, tying with a bow around the waist. Made from ribbon or cord, it sported two long loops at either side that caught a sufficient amount of fabric to elevate the skirt, while afford-

ing the same pleasingly-swaged appearance along the hem. These devices exposed petticoats, which would soon appear in colored versions less indicative of underclothes, and eventually spawned the fashionable "double" skirt (or "overskirt") that became stylish the second half of the decade.

Though skirts were wide they seldom reached the exaggerated proportions (or decorations) illustrated in the popular French fashion plates. The hoops invented in 1856 to accommodate the full skirts of the fifties continued to provide the necessary support underneath. While cumbersome when maneuvering doors and furniture, women welcomed their liberation from the ten or more heavy petticoats previously needed to achieve the same fullness. They also provided immense relief during the hot, humid summer months by allowing air to circulate the lower "limbs," while in the winter, petticoats of flannel or wool could be worn beneath for added warmth. Also called "cage petticoats" or "artificial crinolines," hoops were generally covered by at least one petticoat composed of fluted ruffles or flounced, stiffened muslin. Lower bands could have similar, though separate, padding, all in an effort to hide their presence. When successful, the dress draped gracefully outward into the shape of a triangle. With insufficient covering the bottom hoop was quite evident, and the fabric that fell straight from there to the floor changed the overall silhouette. Hoops that were too short also contributed to this altered appearance, though at least a foot of clearance was required so feet would not become tangled within the steel bands.

Elegant fabric; some sleeve trim; wide pagoda sleeves; rectangular belt buckle. NM

Skirts were normally plain, although a few had a row or two of ruffles at the hem. Sometimes on fancier garments where bodices were trimmed, skirts had like decoration placed horizontally near the bottom to add emphasis to the width. This usually consisted of velvet ribbon placed in rows or shaped into a geometric design. More elaborate garments could be enhanced with a band of black imitation embroidery that had been stamped upon the fabric.

Sleeves

Bodice shoulder fabric continued over the top of the arm where it met diagonally (and sometimes almost horizontally) at the armhole (or "armscye"). The dress tightly enveloped the upper arm before terminating at this seam, which was frequently accented by narrow, fabric-

Very simple garment with coat sleeves. Brownsville, Pennsylvania.

covered string known as "piping." Arm movements were necessarily confined within narrowed limits lest fabric split or be disarranged, and the resulting lack of motion allegedly weakened shoulder and back muscles and even caused tumors. Despite discomfort and possible health risks, the "dropped shoulder" remained a distinctive feature of the sixties, making the shoulders appear sloped and bestowing a demure effect upon the overall costume.

Used exclusively for shirts, though popular alike on bodices, the "bishop" sleeve consisted of a single piece of fabric pleated into the armscye (where it hung very full and loose) and gathered into a narrow wristband. Cut in two pieces with the narrower section situated beneath the arm, the crescent-shaped "coat" sleeve fit smoothly into the armscye, widening at the elbow before narrowing to the wrist, where it turned under in a simple hem. Similar in construction to those used on gentleman's coats, it lent a decidedly "bent elbow" appearance to the wearer. A variant particularly favored the first half of the period consisted of a somewhat shorter rendition. Left wider along the hem to accommodate a bouffant undersleeve, it occasionally displayed deep, turn-back "gauntlet" cuffs. Carried over from the 1850s, the "pagoda" was often reserved for dressier daytime garments. Generally three-quarter length, it widened progressively from the armscye and reached moderate to quite large proportions at the often irregular

hemline. Both open styles were preferred for warm weather, when they naturally provided more ventilation than their closer-fitting counterparts (even with their accompanying undersleeves). The scarce "Pamela" divided the upper sleeve into large puffs and provided a rare diversion from the standard apparel.

Though used sparingly, trim appeared with greater frequency on sleeves than anywhere else upon the garment. It could be placed diagonally below the armscye and above the wristband, vertically down the outer length of the sleeve, or as a decorative edge along the hem of pagodas. Trim was occasionally applied below the armscye to simulate epaulets, or separate fabric caps could be attached—sometimes becoming so enveloping they formed a shallow oversleeve.

Undersleeves, or "engageantes," were universally worn beneath the wider sleeves, adding an elegant touch as they billowed softly from below while effectively hiding the arm from view. Commonly of white, lightweight fabric, though darker colors were utilized during mourning (for collars as well), they formed a tubular shape ranging from narrow to quite full, depending on the type of sleeve they were worn beneath. Open at both ends, undersleeves contained elastic or drawstring to hold them above the elbow and were gathered below into a narrow wristband. This band alone emerged from beneath sleeves that fit snug at the wrist, or deep detachable cuffs that covered the hem might be substituted. Both were effective in protecting the harder-to-clean outer garments from dirt and soil, and when starched, engageantes provided substance to maintain the shape of broader sleeves.

Necklines

Bodice necklines were rounded and came to the base of the neck, where they were often finished along the edge with narrow piping. Stiff, removable white collars of uniform depth generally lay directly on top of the bodice; unless situated perfectly, these untidily exposed fragments of the darker bodice fabric between the collar and neck. (Shirts and Zouaves were supplied in like fashion.) Collars lay flush upon the corsage and either met at the throat, their ends angling moderately outward, or separated slightly to bare a small portion of the bodice. Separate, stubby standing collars were also used. The bodice material could be flat or somewhat upright, with the slightly taller, standing white collar band either emerging from beneath or wrapping around the outside. Illustrations labeled "collars" in fashion magazines frequently displayed the neckwear attached to a chemisette and available in matching sets with undersleeves; however, these were primarily used beneath open-necked garments such as evening wear, V neck jackets (and sometimes Zouaves), less formal morning and home dresses, and the fan-shaped bodices of the elderly. Collars were narrow and commonly quite plain, though fancy lace collars with scalloped edges could ornament finer costumes. Both were often accented by a narrow or medium-sized bow attached at the base of the throat.

Jewelry

In the absence of a bow, a large or small round or oval-shaped brooch was always pinned to the collar. Brooches with black backgrounds were especially popular, often of petra dura, a type of mosaic with flowers or birds so exquisitely cut and set into stone they seemed painted. Cameos enjoyed a popularity that would endure well into the eighties. Garnets and pearls were also stylish, as were hair work ornaments. Women could, with special instruction, fashion hair from loved ones or the "dearly departed" into various forms of jewelry. They also had the option of sending the hair through the mail to firms who, for a price, would do the intricate weaving for them. Watch chains were both ornamental and practical, along with being the most widely used item of jewelry throughout the Victorian period. The long thin chains seldom appeared logically around the neck, however. Instead, they were looped around the belt or suspended from a central button hole in the bodice. When belts were present, watches nestled safely beneath. Otherwise, they reposed in a special tiny pocket situated along the inside edge of the placket and accessed through a narrow vertical slit just below the waistband. Wide gold bangle bracelets (generally supplied in pairs), though occasionally worn, showed to better advantage in the evenings when arms were bared. Wide black bands formed of woven hair, "jet" beads, or a hard, rubber-like substance made from tree sap known as "gutta percha" were far more popular, as they enjoyed greater visibility beneath the white undersleeves. Ears were either unadorned or slender drop earrings graced their pierced lobes (screw backs being an early twentieth-century invention). Simple necklaces and beaded chokers made only rare appearances during the day.

of decorative "snoods" made of ribbon or crochet and frequently enhanced with beads.) A less restricted arrangement seen infrequently featured tightly-wound corkscrew curls, placed either in front or behind the ears, that generally extended to shoulder length.

Hairstyles

Hair was always parted in the center and combed flat on top, where it swept behind, or partially covered, the ears (though ears were fully covered at times). Hair might frame the face with tight, backward rolls, which were often formed over cushions and continued around the neck using the lower portion of the hair—the greater amount above shaped into a bun or additional rolls. Another popular style featured intricate braids beginning above or below the ears that met in back, and from the front the silhouette of both resembled a short (usually reaching between the chin and base of the neck), modern-day page boy. Sometimes hair was crimped, waved, or (more often) drawn smoothly back and loosely confined at the hairline, where it turned under to form a broad "waterfall." A casual, behind-the-ears style featured hair laying smoothly upon the nape, the loose ends turned under and supported by a hair net. (These could be invisible or consist

Fancy sleeve trim; hidden hook and eye bodice closure. NM

Waved hair; watch chain depends from bodice and disappears in placket pocket. Philadelphia, Pennsylvania.

Elegant dress: rare triple flounce on skirt repeated on sleeve; pagoda with scalloped hem; watch chain looped around belt. NM

Trimmed skirt; fancy epaulets; large oval brooch. Lewiston, Maine.

Elegant costume: rare overskirt trimmed to match skirt bottom, sleeves, and long bodice points; lace collar. Watch fits in hidden pocket along bodice waist. Toledo, Ohio. Handwritten date "1863."

Striped dress with trim on sleeves and bodice points. Saratoga Springs, New York.

Polka dot dress with simple trim along skirt bottom and armscye; hoop evident beneath skirt. Woman's hair braided and drawn to back. Concord, New Hampshire. TS canceled in 1864.

Elegant costume: wide pagoda sleeves; flounced, scalloped skirt trim. Boston, Massachusetts.

Bodice trim simulates Zouave jacket;
matching trim along outer sleeve and skirt
hem. Shoulder length, corkscrew curls cover
ears. Winsted, Connecticut.

Elaborate braided trim at top and bottom
of pagodas; wide belt with large
rectangular buckle. Pulaski, New York. TS
canceled April, 1865.

Simple dress has bodice points highlighted. Narrow collar is laid off-center around neckline. Wooster, Ohio. TS

Photographed by ALEXANDER & HODIL, 93 Wood St. Pittsburg.

Bodice trimmed to simulate Zouave; waved hair; wide, matching black bracelets. Pittsburgh, Pennsylvania. TS

Short, corkscrew curls. Elaborate epaulets and cuff trim. Watch chain seen in rare position: around neck! Simple fabric belt closes with hooks and eyes. Pulaski, New York. TS canceled April, 1865.

Elegant print dress with lace collar. Watch depends from central bodice opening and disappears beneath belt. Hoop evident beneath skirt. Columbus, Ohio.

Rare side view. Trim on skirt, bodice points, and sleeves. New York, New York. Handwritten date "June, 1864."

Checked dress; full bishop sleeves; gathered bodice. Black collar and cuffs signify mourning. Black beaded choker. Hair in corkscrew curls behind ears. Albany, New York.

Vertical trim down center bodice matched on sleeves and horizontal trim across chest. NM Handwritten date and location "June, 1863, Mass."

Elegant fabric; pagoda
sleeves with billowing
undersleeves; epaulets so
large they form oversleeve.
Troy, New York. TS

Photd by Schoonmaker
282 River St. Troy, N.Y.

Wide pagoda sleeves trimmed with velvet diamonds, which are repeated on bodice. Prominent black buttons. Hannibal, Missouri.

Large pagoda with epaulette sleeve cap. Black mourning collar and undersleeves. Rounded hem on bodice; hidden hook and eye closure. Philadelphia, Pennsylvania.

Elegant fabric; pagoda decorated with double flounce below armscye. Boston, Massachusetts.

Simple polka dot dress; bishop sleeves; black mourning collar; wide belt with rectangular buckle. Louisiana, Missouri

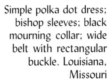

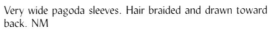
Very wide pagoda sleeves. Hair braided and drawn toward back. NM

Bodice trimmed to simulate Zouave. Watch chain depends from bodice and disappears inside placket pocket. Skirt is fuller toward back. Philadelphia, Pennsylvania.

Simple trim at bodice points and sleeve hem; wide bow at neck; skirt fuller toward back. Watertown, New York.

Rare diagonal closure, edged with trim duplicated on long bodice points, armscye, and sleeve hem. Hairstyle shows width at temples becoming popular by 1864. New York, New York.

Wide pagoda sleeves; Swiss belt. Lowell, Massachusetts.

Bodice with points, worn with matching or simulated Zouave. Short corkscrew curls cover ears. Hazleton, Pennsylvania.

Coat sleeves left wide at the hem appear to have turn-back, gauntlet cuffs. Billowing undersleeves; black bracelet. Hairstyle wide at temples. Brooklyn, New York. Hand dated "April, 1864."

White Garibaldi with trim along central opening and shoulders, accompanied by shawl; separate narrow collar perched on top. Brooklyn, New York.

Garibaldi with full bishop sleeves and matching trim along shoulders, cuffs, and bodice center. Watch chain loops around belt. NM

Plain white shirt; belt; horizontally-striped skirt. Baltimore, Maryland.

Zouave jacket worn with white shirt and polka dot skirt. Philadelphia, Pennsylvania.

Zouave jacket with lace collar placed on top; white shirt; solid skirt. Hair in neat braids pulled toward rear. Lawrence (state not identified).

Zouave jacket worn with white shirt and polka dot skirt. Chatham, New York.

Lady dressed for outdoors with cape, veil, and porte jupe or "dress elevator" disclosing plain white petticoat. NM TS

Chapter Eleven

1865-1868

Not really having a distinct "look," the mid- to late-sixties instead blended attributes from both the preceding and succeeding time periods—though lacking the elegance or grace of either. While subtle changes in the waistline and skirt configuration at first made it difficult to distinguish outfits from the early sixties, later developments such as basques and overskirts lacked the harmony and charm that characterized costumes of the next decade.

Ladies at the left wear simple dresses with rounded false yokes. Both have crimped hair at the temples. The lady to the right wears an overskirt (either real or simulated). Ogdensburg, New York.

Outfits

Skirt fullness at first exceeded the dimensions of the early sixties, with the major expanse concentrated toward the rear and the sides narrowing from hip to hem as the decade progressed. Skirt construction altered to provide a closer fit about the stomach and hips. While large single or double box pleats were helpful in reducing fabric, pronounced goring was even more effective. Fully-gored sections might ease smoothly into the waistband for an especially snug fit (particularly popular toward the end of the period) or incorporate a few pleats at the sides and back. Sometimes skirts with front gores contained full back breadths, which were then constricted by box pleats or gathers.

Skirts were noticeably shorter in front, usually clearing the floor by several inches. By contrast, back lengths trailed upon the ground with a foot or more of fabric. These newly-formed trains spread over hoops that were oval in shape, the fuller portion extending the fabric to the rear. Etiquette dictated that ladies might raise their dresses ankle height with their right hands to clear the streets, but the use of both hands was considered vulgar unless performed fleetingly over excessively muddy ground. To avoid possible censure and more adequately protect delicate fabrics, the porte jupe from the early sixties remained in use. Skirts might also be temporarily or permanently held or "looped" off the floor by intermittently-spaced straps or an arrangement of buttons and loops sewn to the seam of each gore. The festooned hem thus produced exposed the fancy colored petticoat now commonly worn beneath. (A less elegant solution required dividing the train into two sections and then tying them into a low knot!) Gradually, overskirts began to replace looped dresses. These were frequently decorative, however, for the formal underskirt was often left to trail in the dirt. "Walking" dresses of a uniform depth that cleared the ground were introduced in 1867, providing a welcome alternative to the "street sweepers." By 1868, trains were being relegated primarily to carriage, home, and evening use. For added convenience, removable trains joined to a waistband soon became available that could easily convert a walking dress to other purposes.

While the modest single skirt prevailed throughout the period, the new double skirt slowly gained in popularity. Most were quite long, reaching at least three-quarter length. Overskirts could end in points ("Vandykes"), square tabs ("crenelations"), scallops, or graduated steps. A curved apron shape or "tablier" vied with other versions by 1868 and would become the predominant form the last year of the decade and well into the seventies. Overskirts might be a different shade or color than the rest of the garment, and ruffles or velvet ribbons generally accented the hems. Like trim might also appear at the lower edge of single skirts, basques, and sleeves (the trim chosen to enhance one portion repeated throughout); the ribbon of fancier garments might be studded with jet glass or beads. Trim could also simulate an overskirt, thereby saving considerable time and money in the garment's manu-

Square bodice trim; large box pleats on skirt; watch chain loops around belt. Saratoga Springs, New York. TS

facture. Supported only by the hoop, overskirts hung smooth and limp front and back, without all the bunching that would distinguish the early-seventies bustle drapery. As skirts slowly contracted they hugged the hoops more securely, and the steel bands either narrowed or became confined to the lower half to reduce bulk around the hips. Since skirts diminished in length as well as breadth, women no longer seemed to glide upon the surface as in the earlier part of the decade, for the exposure of dainty boots revealed their visible means of locomotion.

Dresses featured snug-fitting, front-buttoning bodices that did not vary greatly in appearance from those of the early sixties except that waists were uniformly rounded. Fabrics too were similar, though with a tendency toward less elegant material for daytime. Solid colors continued to prevail, accompanied by occasional plaids or stripes. False yokes became especially prolific. Simulated by black velvet ribbon, ruffles, or fringe, they could be square-shaped or formed into a curve or W that frequently extended over the armscye. Trim could also be placed vertically upon the bodice in fanciful designs sometimes matched upon the skirt, epaulets, and sleeves. Although referred to as an "empire waist," the waistline was situated only slightly above the natural anatomical placement and was often emphasized by belts featuring large buckles or fabric-formed rosettes. Corsets were laced tightly beneath as narrowed skirts and sleeves no longer provided the illusion of the coveted "wasp" waist.

While the standard corsage remained joined to the skirt, an alternate form revived from the fifties was constructed as a separate entity. Called the "basque" bodice, it extended below the waist to the hips, where large rectangular tabs or pointed Vandykes frequently outlined the hem. Long basques were called "peplums" when they were hollowed front and back, with two longer points at each side. Tassels often accented the extremities of this unusual novelty, which did not appear until the middle of 1866. As the more formal appearance of basques and peplums was often preferred for the street, both were available in removable versions so persons of reduced circumstances might transform a simpler house garment into appropriate street wear. Sometimes, they too were only simulated by the application of trim.

Low, square-cut necklines enclosed by a separate chemisette, advertised as summer wear early in the decade though rarely seen, would continue to be an infrequent feature of the late sixties. Occasionally, bodices featured fabric folded back to form "revers," creating a V neck similarly filled. Though less prolific than in the previous period, the Garibaldi remained fashionable. Plain white waists also continued to be worn with fitted and Zouave jackets or the new sleeveless Spanish (or "bolero") vest. Worn as outer wraps in the early sixties, the loose, thigh-length "sacque" or more fitted "paletot," along with the short, cape-like "pelerine" fashionable by 1868, was often made from the same fabric as the dress, creating a suit-like garment popular summer and winter.

The strong vertical seams produced by the sewing machine made the one-piece dress feasible. Made from gored fabric and lacking a waist seam, it was known interchangeably as the "princess" or "Gabrielle." Introduced at the end of the fifties but only recently receiving much notice for day wear, this smooth, slim-fitting dress commonly buttoned all the way down the front, as, occasionally, did skirts.

Sleeves

The dropped shoulder remained in vogue, continuing to restrict vigorous arm movements, and coat sleeves predominated. Slimmer than those of the early sixties, they retained a slight fullness at the elbow before narrowing to the wrist. There they turned under in a simple hem, often enhanced by the same decorative trim used elsewhere upon the garment. Unless worn beneath the now-scarce, full-length pagoda, the requisite white undersleeve received little exposure excepting the deep wrist band. Epaulets increased in popularity upon the upper arm, either formed by plain or ruffled fabric or simulated by fringe or jet. The bishop remained fashionable for shirts.

Necklines

Bodice necklines resembled those of the early sixties and were rounded or had a slight "stand" at the base of the neck. Their separate white collars were small and narrow, usually featuring fabric that lay flush with the bodice, the ends either angled outward or overlapping. Occasionally collars fit higher, overlapping slightly as they wrapped around the gently-raised neckline. Stubby, white standing collars peeping out from beneath the corsage were also popular and considered especially stylish with their front edges bent to form two points upon the bodice fabric.

Jewelry

Jewelry remained sparse and unobtrusive. Brooches were commonly pinned to the center of the collar. If watch chains were worn, they usually appeared cleverly wrapped about the brooch, hanging straight from there to where the watch rested beneath the belt or within a hidden watch pocket accessed by a small horizontal opening just below the waistband. While necklaces remained unpopular, a preference slowly reemerged for black, choker-style ribbons—which had occasionally appeared above the large collars and slightly-scooped necklines of the fifties and would become especially fashionable by the early seventies. As bracelets rarely surfaced during the day, the only other adornment consisted of the still-popular round or tear-shaped dangling earrings.

Deep, belted basque bodice; beaded epaulets; wide, full skirt trails on floor and buttons center front. Sacramento, California.

Deep basque worn with the very wide skirts popular early in period. San Francisco, California.

Hairstyles

The central part remained standard. From there, hair was often swept tightly behind the ears in a severe mode that disappeared in a tight bun and did nothing to soften or enhance the features. A more stylish look placed emphasis well above the ears in width at the temples. Here it might be formed into "Eugenie" puffs or rolls, which were popularized by the Empress Eugenie of France and began to appear in America around 1864. Wavy bands of hair formed by crimping irons could also radiate from the center part to expand along the temples, receiving added emphasis from the skin-tight hair beneath. The water-fall of the early sixties moved higher upon the back of the head (though some remained low), providing those who utilized it with just enough height at the crown to be flattering. Generally falling no lower than the hairline, the waterfall's basic expanse extended outward, where it could reach quite sizable proportions. False hair pre-formed to the required shape frequently supplemented the overlarge bun—greatly expediting the arrangement of the coiffure. A braid, velvet ribbon, or bow often encircled the waterfall, and two long ringlets formed at the nape and carefully positioned to drape over the shoulder sometimes accompanied the style. A more youthful look featured shoulder-length hair worn down in a cluster of ringlets, held away from the face by combs or a hair band. Though bangs were not fashionable, a few short curls infrequently appeared upon the forehead.

Square bodice trim matched on cuffs and skirt bottom. NM

Fancy trimmed basque bodice. Hair waved at temples. St. Louis, Missouri.

Basque bodice with hem "stepped" progressively downward toward the back. Separate wide skirt buttons center front. San Francisco, California.

Basque displays pointed Vandyke hem and large pagoda sleeves. Fabric-formed rosette at belt. Baltimore, Maryland.

Sleek hairstyle. Trim forms W on bodice.
Fulton, New York.

VAUGHAN'S ENAMELED CARDS,
18 Third Street,
(Late 511 Montgomery St.)   San Francisco.

Fringed "yoke" extends over armscye. Dress has large box pleats along waist and is trained. San Francisco, California.

One-piece princess dress with fancy, braided vertical trim buttons down center front. NM

G. D. Morse,   Phot. S. F.

Plaid dress trails on floor. Hair formed into Eugenie rolls far above ears. San Francisco, California.

G. D. Morse,   Phot. S. F.

Above: Simple trained dress. Hair formed into one long sausage curl positioned over shoulder. San Francisco, California.
Below: Dress with long overskirt (or trimmed to simulate overskirt). Corresponding trim on rounded false yoke and epaulets. Rosette at belt. Corkscrew curls cover ears. Sacramento, California.

Ruffles decorate skirt bottom and rounded false yoke. Fabric rosette at belt. NM

Trim forms W on bodice. Ruffles at hem. Waved hair along temples. West Fairview, Pennsylvania.

Basque bodice shaped in long points. Trim at armscye emphasizes still-popular dropped shoulder. Jamestown, New York.

Long basque (may be detachable). Gores clearly visible on skirt. Very short corkscrew curls. NM

G. D. Morse, 315 Montgomery Street.

Simple dress with square false yoke trim, coat sleeves, and ruffled hem. Watch chain hangs from center brooch—watch plainly visible beneath belt. San Francisco, California.

One-piece princess dress buttons down front. Watch chain hangs from bodice button hole, with watch hiding in small pocket accessed through vertical slit in skirt. Louisville, Kentucky.

Beautiful velvet basque decorated with jet beads. Waved hair at temples. Philadelphia, Pennsylvania.

Zouave jacket with white shirt and shawl. Visible gores on skirt, single ruffle at hem. San Francisco, California.

New York Gallery, 25 Third St. S. F.

Simple dress with velvet trim on cuffs and epaulets. Watch chain suspended from collar brooch. Winsted, Connecticut.

Square-cut bodice filled with separate chemisette. Black choker. Waved, above-the-ears hairstyle. Boston, Massachusetts.

ENAMELED CARDS, FROM
C. L. CRAMER'S CALIFORNIA GALLERY,
Cor. Pine and Kearny Streets, S. F.

Basque bodice trimmed with ruffle matched on epaulets and rounded false yoke. Long trained skirt trails on floor. Waved hair typifies width at temples. San Francisco, California.

Fringe decorates scalloped hem of overskirt and rounded false yoke on bodice. Bodice folds in at the neck and is supplemented by chemisette. Black choker. Hair waved at temples with single sausage curl. Albany, New York.

Scalloped overskirt in lighter fabric than underskirt. Black choker above large neck ribbon. Boonville, New York.

Narrow velvet trims sleeve and square "yoke." Double flounce at hem. Rosette "buckle" emphasizes slightly-raised Empire waistline. Narrow collar wraps around bodice neckline. NM

Simple outfit with epaulets, trimmed at hem with double flounce. Skirt fits smoothly into waistband and has narrowed considerably from earlier in the period. San Jose, California.

Vertical trim simulates overskirt; rosette at belt. San Francisco, California.

Lovely ensemble features matching overskirt and pelerine. Sacramento, California.

Chapter Twelve

1869-1875

Overskirts elegantly draped over an elaborate bustle replaced the limp styles of the late sixties. Hair appeared in more abundance and luxuriant abandon than at any other time in the nineteenth century. While bodices still fit fairly snug on the upper torso, loose sleeves and basques combined with full skirts, ruffles, and bouffant drapery to result in a brief period where the desire for a wasp waist was superseded by a look more charming than slenderizing. This was the height of the feminine era, where ruffles and frills abounded, and hair gently framed the face in a profusion of flattering styles.

Ornamental ruche defines edge of basque over simulated vest. Lots of ruffles and trim; wide, striped and frayed cravat; black choker. Huge chignon rests against forehead. Stockton, California.

Outfits

The most popular form of dress consisted of the hiplength basque, alternately referred to as a jacket-style bodice, which was worn with a separate skirt and overskirt. Basques could be of uniform depth or form single or double points in front, and earlier styles sometimes included a belt. The rear portion could be of equal depth, but more often it formed an elongated "postillion" that rested upon the bustle. Bodices fastened down the center front, often with large buttons that stood out prominently, and were sometimes trimmed to simulate an open jacket over a shorter vest. Though some ease existed in the fit, boning was still required to maintain the shape. The small waspish waist was for a fleeting time less fashionable, and it was even suggested that those unfortunate women who had attained their tiny waists after much personal suffering and injury might now require padding to be in style! Corsets were of course worn, but more for support than constriction.

Shirts made an infrequent appearance, accompanied by a short, waist-length vest or longer, close-fitting "sleeveless basque." The latter was often elegantly fashioned of velvet and might also grace the standard bodice. A longer basque known as the "cuirass" was introduced around mid-decade, and it alone would dominate the second half of the seventies. A vertical, rectangular-shaped "plastron" filled with contrasting fabric frequently divided the front of this elongated garment.

Overskirts were typically formed into a knee-length, apron-shaped drape. Fabric fell smoothly upon the skirt below or was perhaps lightly creased by a few sporadically-placed tackings along the sides (all elaboration, however, was reserved for the bouffant back drapery). The overskirt could be raised at the thighs or pulled directly toward the rear. Tapes sewn to the side seams underneath tied invisibly behind the thighs to hold fabric smooth and flat. Sometimes the front and rear portions were constructed individually and then joined at the waistband. Overskirts were often separate entities that were simply placed on top of the underskirt; in rare instances, they were absent altogether.

The "polonaise" (referred to less often as a "tunic" or "casaque") became a stylish alternative to the skirt and basque. Consisting of a combination bodice and overskirt, it lacked a waist seam and was worn over a separate underskirt. Early styles featured split skirts with tight hems that caused the gathered fabric within to puff about the hips into "panniers" reminiscent of the eighteenth century. A specially-designed horsehair bustle padded these side pouches along with the derriere. A far more prevalent polonaise formed the apron-shaped tablier, which often buttoned all the way down the front, sometimes double breasted. In a popular variation, the "apron" unbuttoned at or slightly below the waist, where it fell open to reveal the underskirt (this version was sometimes worn long, extending all the way to mid-calf). A simi-lar style eliminated buttons from the lower half, with the central portion folded back to form revers or narrowed into two long points at either side. The polonaise could also resemble a long basque with a simulated vest, alternately termed a "jacket with extended basques." Similar versions were called "redingotes" because of their resemblance to a gentleman's riding coat. Usually fashioned from heavier materials, these often sufficed for a jacket in the winter. While the polonaise generally looped up at the sides, it sometimes remained of uniform depth or became elongated toward the back. Like the basque, it too could be worn with or without a belt or sash and was available in a rare sleeveless version.

Underskirts fastened at the back and remained gored in front, where they hung straight and smooth. Some fullness was retained at the sides, with the major expanse concentrated in the full rectangular back breadths, which were constricted by pleats or gathers. (This combination of front gores and full back widths became the standard method throughout the seventies and eighties for maintaining a smooth fit about the stomach and hips while producing excess material directly below the waist in back.) The underskirt was largely hidden by the overskirt, whose fabric was variously contrived

---

Ruffles accent overskirt hem and form square yoke that continues over armscye. Deep flounce on underskirt. Hair pulled away from ears and hangs freely down the back. St. Louis, Missouri.

---

over the newly-fashionable bustle or "tournure." The hem of the overskirt could consist of a tight band, which caused the excess gathered fabric to "pouf" or balloon over the derriere—a form particularly stylish during the first half of the period. Fabric could also lay gracefully upon the rounded bustle or, more popularly, be bunched into elegant drapery. This effect was created beneath by vertical tapes, which depended from the waistband and were buttoned, tacked, or hooked at irregular intervals to hold the raised, bulging folds of fabric in place. An arrangement of "buttons and loops" might also regulate fabric (such temporary measures greatly aiding the laundering process)! Some draperies were so intricate ladies sometimes misdirected the folds—especially upon newer garments! Though bustles were usually separate entities, skirts were occasionally equipped with a built-in framework consisting of several semicircular hoops and a pad.

Overskirts generally ended midway upon the back of the underskirt. At times, however, they could mingle with, or replace, an underskirt that altered the more rounded appearance of the silhouette by continuing outward into a moderate train. This appendage continued to pose a problem for ladies, as soiling skirts remained preferable to the indiscretion of raising them above ankle height. Innumerable mechanisms were devised to allow retention of elegant trains while avoiding dusty streets. Waistbands could be equipped underneath with vertical tapes ending in hooks or buttonholes that, when attached to "eyes" or buttons sewn near the hem, effectively lifted fabric above street level. Another device allowed for the quick raising or lowering of the train as needed. It consisted of two cords passed through a series of rings attached to the inner side seams and ultimately protruding through holes at either end of the waistband. When pulled tight and fastened, the cords elevated the sides of the skirt and with them the protracted back lengths. Longer trains required threading a single cord through rings placed in a semicircle about half way down the skirt's underside. When drawn, the overskirt conveniently concealed the resultant bunching of fabric at the derriere. Many women were not overly concerned about their trailing appendages, however, as they were often left to sweep upon dirty roads and sidewalks, protected only by an inner facing of oil cloth, "plaited wigging," braided morocco, or a trained petticoat. Or, the dilemma could be

Unusual ensemble contains contrasting overskirt with belted basque. San Francisco, California.

avoided altogether by those who chose to wear the shorter, train-less "walking" dresses, which shared equal popularity with their dust-gathering counterparts throughout the period.

Underskirts were generally plain or had a single wide ruffle at the hem. Less often, the entire exposed surface could be decorated with flounces or perhaps alternating rows of ruffles and pleats. Ruffles or other decorative trim generally edged the hem of the basque, polonaise, and overskirt as well. While trim could be purchased to a limited extent ready-made, it was usually laboriously constructed and attached with the aid of the sewing machine—by now an affordable commodity for most upper and middle class families. Bodice surfaces could be plain but were more often enhanced by a narrow band of trim known as a "ruche." Formed of fabric gathered on running center or parallel stitches or fashioned into widely-spaced knife or box pleats (occasionally double-edged), this popular garnish appeared around V necks, as a single row of vertical trim on either side of the bodice, or to help define the "edge" of a polonaise or bodice incorporating a false vest. The square and rounded yoke designs, so popular upon the upper bodice in the late sixties, lingered into the early seventies, joined by a V shape also formed of fringe or lace. Only one trim at a time was generally utilized over the entire garment, and while frills and ruffles abounded, they were beautifully coordinated and seldom overburdening.

Outfits were predominantly composed from a single, solid-colored light or dark fabric, though two contrasting hues, or stripes,

were sometimes used. The seldom seen "Dolly Varden" emerged during the second half of the period and featured a polonaise made from printed fabric known as chintz, worn over a solid-colored skirt.

Sleeves

The armscye was often accented with thick piping and could remain dropped or reach as high as the point of the shoulder, where it combined with fuller sleeves to at last free the arm for a wider range of motion. Loose fitting, full-length coat sleeves were popular—either ending in a coordinating ruche or in deep cuffs heavily ornamented with tucks, pleats, and overlarge buttons. Some sleeves were further ornamented by a small puff of gathered fabric that terminated several inches below the shoulder in a band of complementing trim. Seen only sporadically during the late sixties, pagoda sleeves again became popular. Almost full length, they flared gradually from the armscye, attaining moderate to quite large proportions at the wrist, where they were usually trimmed with a single or double row of ruffles, fringe, or lace. Occasionally a shorter pagoda was worn, with tighter sleeves of the same fabric beneath. Similar in appearance, the "bell" sleeve fit snug to the elbow, where it then flared out about the lower arm.

Engageantes remained in use, but despite the opportunity again afforded by wider sleeves, they were no longer full and bouffant. Instead, deep cuffs were generally all that was discernible. Sleeves might also be edged simply underneath with a narrow border of white lace, allowing bare skin to be visible when the arms were raised. Sometimes deep, detachable white inner cuffs accommodated closer-fitting sleeves, disclosing only a small portion from where they were basted beneath.

Necklines

Though necklines lowered, the daytime decolletage bared, at most, only a shallow narrow section of the upper chest. In fact, this was as daring as daytime apparel would get for the remainder of the Victorian period. Plain round necks that came to the base of the throat, or

Basque bodice incorporates simulated vest. Front portion of overskirt hangs flat in front and is constructed separately from the back, the two then joined at the waistband. Chagrin Falls, Ohio.

V necklines, sometimes edged with a ruche of knife or box pleats or having a turn-down collar or lapels, were the standard—with square necklines reserved mostly for evening wear. Open necklines increased the use of chemisettes, and their decorative white standing ruffles or pleats rose engagingly from beneath to further enclose the chest. Higher, rounded necklines were enhanced by a narrow, white, "pie-crust" frill sewn to the inside or attached to a small dickey. While ruffles were especially favored, an occasional plain inner collar band with a shallow "stand" to the back, whose narrow ends often folded over the bodice front in late sixties-style, could be attached to a foundation or merely inserted within the bodice neckline and tacked in place. Or, small to medium-sized linen or lace collars that widened as they approached the throat might be placed directly on top of the corsage. Less often, a piece of lace or a narrow, ruffled "fraise" was substituted, positioned on top of the bodice and attaching at the base of the throat. As an added embellishment, wide neck ribbons called "cravats" were especially popular, either overlapped or tied into a bow. These incorporated stripes, checks, or light-colored fabrics whose ends were generally flattened upon the chest and either embroidered with flowers or frayed along the edge.

Jewelry

The feminine nature expressed in ruffles and unfettered locks extended to a more noticeable display of jewelry. As lower necklines left the entire throat area exposed, the most prominent ornament consisted of a black ribbon choker, worn plain or with a locket or cross suspended from its center. This was often accompanied by either a necklace or a watch chain. Watch chains were fairly thick and generally found hanging from the neck or looped around the collar brooch. Necklaces could be quite conspicuous, made from large jet beads or enormous chain links, with a huge gold or gutta percha cross or locket attached (though small lockets on thin chains were also seen). Chains and beads might be so long they wrapped first about the throat before falling upon the bosom. Brooches were commonly pinned to collars and cravats. Made en suite with long earrings, their ornate shapes were frequently enhanced by dangling centers and enameled engraving called "taille d' epergne." Though bracelets were seldom visible, wide black bangles continued to display best beneath the long sleeves. Such jeweled abundance was not without its critics, who condemned society for its ostentatious love of display and corresponding lack of refinement.

Hairstyles

Hairstyles were distinctive due to their lack of confinement. Hair appeared with great profusion in a variety of flattering styles. It could be parted in the center and swept away from the face, with clips or hair ribbons holding it securely until it tumbled freely about the shoulders or in a mass of long sausage curls. Or it could simply be pulled back and confined at the nape into a long "tail" that often extended to the waist and beyond, with the fancy top of a tortoise shell comb sometimes visible at the crown. The most popular style featured a central part, the hair drawn into an enormous braided "chignon" (or bun) placed only an inch or so from the forehead and covering the entire crown. In a similar variation, the front hair swept over the chignon, covering the sides and leaving only the braided center exposed. (Occasionally a hair band positioned flat upon the head, tiara fashion, replaced the chignon.) Hair might be confined entirely within the bun or a portion could escape down the back unfettered or in carefully composed sausage curls. Hairstyles always left the ears bared, and while the center part was most common, hair could also be parted at the side or combed directly back from the face. Bangs were not especially fashionable, though a few short wisps upon the forehead were fairly common. The look of bangs could also be contrived from hair parted in the center and held firm within a hair band or bun, each side then drawn down to form a loop. There was also a fad for a fringe of tightly-wound corkscrews, and these were often supplied by false hair, making it unnecessary to cut bangs. It was the large chignon, however, that created the greatest demand from a burgeoning industry that would continue, throughout the Victorian period, to produce hair of all shapes and sizes to meet the needs of prevailing fashions.

Left: Plaid ensemble with shallow overskirt and triple flounces beneath. Black choker with large locket; lace fichu. Mobile, Alabama.

Center: Belted basque lacks overskirt. Large pagoda sleeves match undersleeves, which also have separate white under cuffs. NM

Right: Knee-length polonaise decorated with bows and raised just slightly at the side; matching ruche down front and hem, along cuffs of bell sleeves, and above deep flounce of underskirt. Lace collar widens toward throat. NM

Attractive striped outfit has full pagodas over matching undersleeves and a flat, stripped bow at the base of a deep lace collar. Standard black choker surrounds neck. Troy, New York.

Simple checked dress is certainly not elegant, yet it is in the current style. Appleton, Wisconsin.

Large woman wears simple basque with hem trim matching that on over- and underskirt. Cravat at neck. NM

Prominent, pie-crust frill; large, round, dangling jet earrings. Deep, turn-back cuffs; matching ruffle edges over- and underskirt flounce. Philadelphia, Pennsylvania.

76

Attractive outfit with lots of coordinating, ruffled trim. Placerville, California.

Simple ruche formed by fabric gathered on running center stitch outlines pagoda sleeves, basque, and overskirt—which achieves light creasing by two tackings along the sides. Black choker with small, heart-shaped locket; large cravat frayed along edges. San Francisco, California.

Opposite Page

Plaid blouse worn under waist-length vest. Hair pulled from bun into two prominent loops upon forehead. San Francisco, California.

Lace enhances square false yoke and hem of bell sleeves, basque, and overskirt. Watch chain hangs from brooch and disappears inside central opening near bosom. San Francisco, California.

Prominent bustle; trained underskirt; matching undersleeves beneath wide pagodas; separate white under cuffs; wide, black choker. San Francisco, California.

New York Gallery, 25 Third St. S. F.

Left:
Trained ensemble abounds in ruffles. Upper sleeves feature small puff edged with ruffle. St. Louis, Missouri.

Right:
Pleated ruche around basque neckline further enhanced by full, white standing ruffles. Flattened cravat ends embroidered with flowers. Napa, California.

Elaborate ensemble features velvet plastron outlined with Vandykes and partially covered by deeply-fringed cravat. Huge braided chignon entirely covers head. Long, dangling earrings. San Francisco, California.

CRAMER, PHOTO.   SAN FRANCISCO.

Long polonaise has box-pleated ruche around neck and revers accenting divided overskirt. Underskirt decorated with alternating rows of pleats and ruffles. Bay City, Michigan.

Gibson, Center Street, Bay City, Mich.

Fringed overskirt of contrasting fabric complements fringed cravat. San Francisco, California.

Very wide, trained underskirt. Black choker above wide cravat. Large braid placed close to forehead. New York, New York.

Very simple basque, over- and underskirt ensemble with ruffled trim. Large cravat. San Francisco, California.

Revered basque over what may be separate vest. Wide, double-pleated cuffs with plain white under cuffs. San Francisco, California.

Aunt Matt

Mora

707 BROADWAY.

Top Left:

Deep cuffs; prominent buttons surrounded by box-pleated ruche; standing inner collar band bends horizontally in front. Center-parted hair partially covers tiara-positioned headband. San Francisco, California.

Top Right:

Huge buttons ornament polonaise. Large cuffs match decorative pocket. Prominent white, pie-crust frill emerges from neckline. Narrow collarette encircles bodice neck, ending in lace bow. Elaborate, sloping bustle. New York, New York.

CRAMER, PHOTO.   SAN FRANCISCO

Bottom Left:

Simple polonaise has large bodice buttons and revers on divided overskirt. Hairstyle features tiara-style headband and long black ringlets. San Francisco, California.

Bottom Right:

Large buttons highlight cuffs and bodice. Polonaise front divides into narrow points and is raised along sides by deep tabs. Huge braided chignon reaches forehead. San Francisco, California.

82

Separate, sleeveless velvet basque worn above standard basque; white, ruffled fraise placed above bodice neckline. Black choker sports large locket; thick watch chain around neck. Petaluma, California.

Below:

Elaborate ensemble features modest pagoda sleeves, lots of lace and ruffles, and full sloping bustle. White neck frill helps enclose V neck. San Francisco, California.

Sleeveless velvet basque worn over separate shirt (or basque)? Low V neck with center properly filled by white ruffles. Parted hair covers sides of large braided chignon. Virginia, Nevada.

Probably sisters, this lady appears to be dressed identically to the previous photo. Note placement of watch within ruffled, trimmed hem of basque. San Francisco, California.

Simple but lovely striped, bustled ensemble.
Flattened, embroidered cravat. Sutter Creek,
California.

This lady has perfected the slightly forward-tilting
"Grecian bend" stance. Jet-studded black lace
highlights; white lace collar; stiff, white inner cuffs.
Santa Cruz, California.

HODSON, - - - - PHOTOGRAPHER.
SANTA CRUZ, CAL.

Left:

Older lady wears stylish ensemble featuring
knife-pleated ruche along either side of
center closure. San Francisco, California.

Right:

Older lady in very elaborate, lace-trimmed
outfit. Square neckline filled by separate
chemisette; wide pagoda sleeves. Watch
hides beneath belt. Hair in braided chignon
with two long sausage curls. New York,
New York.

Lovely white bustled ensemble with trained underskirt.
Black choker. Hair in long flattering ringlets. San Francisco,
California.

Heavily-trimmed outfit with deep overskirt. Hair
displays vertical rolls characteristic of succeeding
period. San Francisco, California.

Though abundantly trimmed, outfit begins to show
attributes popular during the late seventies: long
overskirt, cuirass bodice, and large side pocket.
Chicago, Illinois.

Chapter Thirteen

1876-1878

The middle to late seventies witnessed the gradual progression of the fashionable silhouette toward a vertical outline as outfits became more form fitting. Though named after the breastplate on a suit of armor, the recently-introduced cuirass bodice did not at this time detract from the feminine look that, due to the slight fullness of the skirts, graceful trains, and flattering hairdos, still prevailed in modified form from the early seventies. The overall appearance resembled a slimmer, more subdued version—minus the ruffles and bustles—of the preceding period.

Outfits

Competing with other styles since its introduction in 1874, the cuirass emerged as the sole form of bodice. The cuirass was a front-buttoning, long-waisted, tightfitting boned bodice that extended below the hips (though many examples had some "give" in this area). It was made without a waist seam and could be hemmed all one length or dip to a curve or point front and back, where it then rose in gentle or extreme arches over the hips. Resembling the cuirass from the front, a similar garment called a "Directoire" contained long coat tails reaching all the way to the floor. Tight lacing returned and corsets lengthened to accommodate the deeper basque. To help lessen the bulk beneath the form-fitting garments, "combination" underclothes were devised uniting the chemise and drawers or corset cover and petticoat.

Overskirts followed the lead of basques and lengthened substantially at mid-decade. Eighteen seventy-five witnessed short basques and overskirts worn side by side with the newer, longer versions. By 1876 the transformation was complete, and overskirts reaching anywhere from mid-calf to only a few inches above the underskirt complemented the cuirass. On rare occasions the apron or newer square-shaped appendage was omitted or so prolific that two identically-shaped overskirts were worn. Skirts beneath narrowed considerably. While goring limited material in front, the full back breadths were drawn together not only at the waist but behind the thighs. There an arrangement of string or elastic, with or without benefit of casings, held the skirt close to the body. Sitting became difficult unless accomplished sideways and even then needed to be performed carefully, lest the restricting bands give way.

The basque and skirt steadily lost favor to the one-piece dress. Designed especially for Princes Alexandra, this version became known exclusively as the "princess." Though the polonaise continued to be worn, it lengthened to the extent that it was often barely distinguish-

Two sisters wear matching princess polonaise dresses with diagonal closures. Lady in center wears striped princess polonaise with fringed hem over solid, dark-colored underskirt. Sacramento, California.

legs. Bustles lingered in modified versions until even these lost their appeal by 1877. The skirt retained some breadth from the early seventies, though this would diminish gradually as the decade progressed. Most fullness was concentrated toward the rear. Starting lower now, at thigh level, fabric began a gradual descent outward, where it slowly fanned into a luxurious train somewhat resembling a peacock trailing its tail. Back lengths could retain the drapery effect produced by inner tapes or fall smoothly toward the floor, accented perhaps by a large bow. Starched petticoats heavily flounced in back provided the sole support. (A cooler summertime alternative consisted of lightweight steels suspended low from vertical tapes in a type of inverse tournure.) Now considered an indispensable part of the overall costume, trains became standard for day wear. While smaller "demi" trains existed, most were quite long. Because of their narrowness and excessive weight, caused by over- and underskirt fabrics and trim, it was no longer as feasible to raise them mechanically above street level. Since dust and mud were thus unavoidable, dresses were protected from becoming too bedraggled by a wide border of stiff muslin known as a "balayeuse."

Two identically-dressed young ladies (probably sisters). Cuirass fits loosely over hips and is trimmed with fringe similar to skirt bottom. Skirts are tacked near hem (to imitate overskirt)? Watch fits in special pocket near waist—chain hangs around neck. Reading, Pennsylvania.

able from the longer dress (hence its frequent reference as a "princess polonaise"). Differentiating between the genuine article and the copy became difficult, especially when applied trim simulated a tablier upon the one-piece garment. For practical reasons the polonaise became preferred for street wear, as it was easier to replace a torn or begrimed underskirt than an entire dress. Excess trim seldom interrupted the smooth lines of the long garments, and the slim-fitting dresses were quite elegant in their simplicity—along with being rather figure-revealing. Both generally closed down the center front with buttons that extended anywhere from the middle to the bottom of the skirt. In rare instances they could fasten diagonally or at the back, where inverted pleats were commonly used to draw fabric in at the waist, allowing it to expand from there into an elegant drape. An inner tie or belt called a "petersham" also helped mold the dress to the figure (and was commonly employed throughout the Victorian era upon bodices as well).

Skirts continued to close in back and were held flat in front by tapes that attached to the side seams underneath and tied behind the

Cuirass with coat sleeves fits loose over hips. Long overskirt; train. Petaluma, California.

This handy article was basted beneath the hem for easy removal and laundering, allowing it to accommodate any number of dresses. It also facilitated walking by preventing skirts from becoming tangled between the ankles.

Ladies' arms largely replaced drawstrings to raise and lower trains, and fashion periodicals went to great lengths regarding management of the flowing appendage. The proper elevating technique involved a glance over the shoulder while bending backward as the right hand reached low to gather up the fabric, which was then held in the hand or draped over the arm. To free both hands for carrying parcels or other necessities, the right arm could be passed through a special ribbon loop attached to the train. Both methods were so effective that skirts were often raised immodestly above the ankles, and while the back was temporarily relieved of its burden, the weight was instead transferred to the arm and shoulder. Though a nuisance, dragging in the dirt and frequently getting stepped on or heavy and cumbersome if carried in order to prevent the aforementioned circumstance, trains nonetheless presented an elegant appearance many ladies were loathe to relinquish. A battle raged throughout 1878 over elimination of the clumsy, dirt-gathering articles, and much to the relief of more practical-minded women, who anxiously awaited their demise, a few trainless options slowly began to emerge.

As in the early seventies, solid light- or dark-colored fabrics predominated. Garments were sometimes constructed of two contrasting materials—one often forming the popular plastron, which was frequently defined by piping along the edge. Velvet and satin were the preferred fabrics to confine within and were also used to fashion vertical rows of bodice trim, sleeves, collars, cuffs, or a decorative band placed diagonally across the skirt or horizontally near the hem. Outfits were often quite plain, however, with ornamentation concentrated on the lower portion of the skirt and overskirt. Except for bows and loose horizontal folds, which could be found sporadically placed down the entire front length of the skirt, decorations such as ruffles, knife or box pleats, lace, fringe, and tassels were generally limited to the hem of the skirt, overskirt, and train (with corresponding trim ornamenting the lower edge of the basque, if worn). Occasionally, the polonaise could end in fancy scallops or Vandykes. Large ornamental pockets placed midway down the side of the skirt were also quite stylish, as well as practical for tight skirts, making prominent an object which standard Victorian practice kept hidden within the side seams. Often only a solitary pocket was visible, reflecting the asymmetry beginning to creep into garments. Diagonal closures and off-centered swaged or square-shaped overskirts, frequently highlighted by buttons or bows, also revealed this trend.

Sleeves

Armhole seams were now at the point of the shoulder and frequently emphasized with piping. Full-length coat sleeves still fit slightly loose, capped by decorative, triangular-shaped cuffs often ornamented by a large bow or medium-sized, diagonally-placed buttons. Piping commonly outlined the cuff, which ended in a row or two of wide knife pleats flaring upon the wrist. Narrow engageantes with deep, plain bands continued in use, but simple detachable white cuffs or a lacy frill more often appeared basted beneath the sleeve.

Necklines

Though an occasional ruche of knife pleats lingered from the early seventies to decorate the bodice around the neck, most were plain. Necklines were no longer "revealing." Bodices now had moder-

Long princess polonaise with prominent, pie-crust frill. Pekin, Illinois.

Long fringed cuirass and overskirt; large neck bow. Reading, Pennsylvania.

Deep cuirass with plastron front; tiny cuff pin rests upon sleeve. Skirt has sporadic tucks and ends in crenelations. Winona (state not identified).

ate-sized standing collars that framed the neck from behind but often dipped slightly in front, sometimes bending horizontally as they exposed the throat. Prominent white, pie-crust frills appeared from beneath, either basted or attached to a dickey. Plain white standing bands were less favored and usually bent lightly over the front portion of the collar, which might be accented by a large flat bow. Long, frilly jabots were also popular—either attached separately at the base of the collar or included as part of a "collarette," which noticeably encircled the dress collar with its flat, lacy white band. Narrow fringed bows might also be tied around the neck.

Jewelry

Jewelry continued to be popular, though long, closer-fitting sleeves discouraged the wearing of bracelets, and higher necklines no longer favored chokers. Watch chains, however, grew in popularity and continued to reside around the neck or the collar brooch. Generally fashioned from thick links, they often sported large ornate slides decorated with stone cameo centers. The watches themselves rested in tiny pockets near the waistline, which were accessed through a horizontal slit or, more popularly, exposed upon the outside of the garment and occasionally made even more distinct by contrasting fabric. In their absence thick necklaces were often worn. Constructed of mesh or from round or box-shaped links, they usually featured short center extensions supporting large engraved and enameled lockets. Exposed ears still sported dangling earrings that often matched the brooches perched upon jabots—unless these had been replaced by the newly-emerging bar pins. Small gold cuff pins occasionally provided a barely-perceptible ornament upon the sleeves.

Hairstyles

Hairstyles remained flattering and, though more confined, resembled those of the early seventies. Hair continued to be braided and coiled into a hot, heavy bun, though it was not quite as large or placed as close to the forehead. A more contemporary look featured hair shaped into large rolls situated horizontally or vertically upon the top of the head. In rare instances when hair was worn flat, fancy combs were usually inserted at the crown to give the illusion of height. Hair was either parted in the center and drawn back or fashioned into short wispy, frizzed, or curled bangs. If any tresses fell below the hairline, they were confined within a few sausage curls draped gracefully over the shoulder or formed into a single braided loop that rested upon the nape.

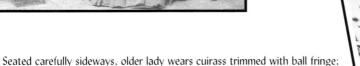

Princess polonaise with diagonal closure. Inner white standing band bends lightly over upright bodice collar. Hairstyle features vertical rolls and two long sausage curls over shoulder. Auburn (state not identified).

Seated carefully sideways, older lady wears cuirass trimmed with ball fringe; ruffled over- and underskirt. Canton, Pennsylvania.

Wedding photo. Orange blossoms; long veil; cuirass with
simulated vest. St. Louis, Missouri.

Cuirass; white fichu; long overskirt with large pocket and shallow train. NM

Wedding photo. Orange blossoms; long veil; deep cuirass raised at hips and decorated with same fringe as long overskirt. Chicago, Illinois.

Smith 214 ESSEX ST., SALEM.

Deep cuirass raised at the hips and enhanced with velvet sleeves and bodice design. Large braided bun set back from forehead. Salem, Massachusetts.

Long princess polonaise decorated with sporadic tucks below hips and ending in tassel-trimmed Vandykes. Bow tops long train. Inner collar dips over that of bodice. San Francisco, California.

Cuirass; triangular-shaped cuffs; large side pocket on overskirt; train. San Francisco, California.

Simple skirt lacks overskirt and is worn with loose-fitting cuirass. Watch enters horizontal slit near waist to reach inner pocket. Hair formed into horizontal rolls. San Francisco, California.

Bodice fastens in back; neckline features white, pie-crust frill surrounded by black lace collarette. Large cuffs ornamented with Vandykes, knife pleats, and lace. Short, curly fringe and large bun. Mok Hill, California.

Princess polonaise enhanced with bows and sporadic tucks. Cuff is outlined in piping, ornamented with buttons and bows, and ends in knife pleats. Collarette encircles neck. San Jose, California.

Armhole seams reach shoulder point and are emphasized with piping. Collar of cuirass folded into two points and enhanced by large cameo. Thick watch chain encircles neck. Double row of knife pleats frame wrist. San Francisco, California.

Cuirass dips low in front, raises over hips. No overskirt. Long trained underskirt features tucks and bows and ends in box pleats. Short curled bangs with long sausage curl. NM

Velvet highlights watch pocket, triangle-shaped cuff, and band near hem of princess (or princess polonaise?) dress. Fringed bow around neck. Sacramento, California.

Cuirass bodice; overskirt trimmed with wide diagonal band; fringed bow tied around neck. Santa Rosa, California.

Long trained princess dress. San Francisco, California. Photo imprinted "November, 1877."

Striped princess dress features solid-colored sleeves, black lace collarette and skirt trim. Braided bun with long sausage curls. San Francisco, California.

Very simple princess dress ornamented with large side pocket and hem trim. San Francisco, California.

Cuirass with velvet sleeves and plastron. Overskirt trimmed with velvet Vandykes and tassels. Underskirt and train have triple flounce. Thick necklace features center extension. Los Angeles, California.

Long deep basque with plastron and fringe trim. New York, New York. Hand dated "October, 1878." (Celebrity)

MARIE ROZE.

707 BROADWAY, N.Y.

Elite 838 MARKET ST.

Side view of bustle-less skirt with long, narrow train. San Francisco, California.

Long cuirass ends in black lace, as does overskirt. Lace also decorates neckline of plaid cuirass and peeps from beneath knife pleats along wrist. San Francisco, California.

Back-fastening princess polonaise (or princess?) ends in fancy scallops. Bar pin rests at collar base. San Jose, California.

Long snug cuirass with vertical trim. Deep overskirt graced by sporadic tucks. Short wispy fringe and three vertical rolls placed well back from forehead. Sacramento, California.

Deep, slim-fitting cuirass. Cuffs decorated with buttons, scallops, and knife pleats. Necklace with center extension. San Francisco, California.

Overskirt features large pocket and button-formed tucks with corresponding drapes of fabric. Fringed cuirass further decorated with vertical trim. Large bow at neck. Hair formed into three large vertical rolls. San Francisco, California. Hand dated "December, 1877."

Simple princess polonaise (or princess?) with plastron. Skirt ends in pointed tabs and lacks train. San Francisco, California.

Princess dress shows signs on skirt of more elaborate decoration characteristic of succeeding time period. San Francisco, California.

Chapter Fourteen

1879-1882

As the eighties approached the slenderizing that began after mid-decade reached its apex, with skirts hanging straight and close at the sides, front, and back, rendering an overall stick-like appearance. The distinguishing feature was the seemingly endless variety of decorative elements incorporated within the costumes. Never had such an abundance of ornament flourished upon everyday garments. Yet in spite of elegant fabrics and elaborate trim, the softness that lingered during the second half of the seventies began to fade. Close-fitting outfits and restrictive hairstyles created a more severe aspect, as if everything on the body had been pulled tight.

Outfits

The long, snug-fitting cuirass bodice still prevailed, though shorter basques were again beginning to emerge. The cuirass could be hemmed evenly (sometimes curving into a W at center front) or formed into single, double, and occasionally even triple or quadruple points. The back might be of like depth or contain longer postilions. A back-lacing, sweater-like garment called a "jersey" was introduced at this time but gave the cuirass little competition, for it so surpassed even that figure-mold-

W. A. Fermann, Stoughton, Wis.

Plastrons and flounced, accordion-pleated underskirts highlight garments of seated ladies. Stoughton, Wisconsin.

inner design would not be marred. Shirring was especially fashionable. Formed by a running stitch sewn in parallel rows and then pulled into small decorative puffs of fabric, it became prolific enough at times to encompass the entire bodice. "Smocking" (or "gauging") was also used, creating a honeycomb pattern very similar in appearance. Jet beads, first introduced as a clothing trim in the mid-fifties, became quite popular throughout the eighties to ornament both skirt and bodice. Occasionally a short, cape-like pelerine hid the bodice altogether, forming an integral part of an outfit sometimes referred to as a "pilgrimage costume" in contemporary pattern books.

The princess dress again receded from fashion and the polonaise became most favored. The polonaise was now a snug-fitting garment with its distinctive overskirt usually ending half to three-quarters distance down the skirt. While the upper section of the polonaise (sometimes appearing in "basque style with draperies added") was decorated in like fashion as the separate bodice and could often be quite plain, the overskirt appeared in an astonishing variety of shapes. The most popular configuration formed an inverted V, which was variously displayed by the follow-

ing styles. Reviving again the popular eighteenth-century fashion, panniers less bouffant than the seventies were formed by fabric that met at the center front and then curved behind the thighs—an inner lining of crinoline or stiffened muslin sustaining its slight pouch along the hips. A similar fashion could bunch at the hips, pannier-style, or appear in longer lengths that fit more smoothly, where it was sometimes termed a casaque. Both versions rose at center front, often gathered in a vertical seam terminating with a bow, separating from

ing article only the boldest women dared wear it. These form-fitting garments became so constricting that the elongated corsets beneath often cracked from being adjusted too tightly, demanding that stronger materials such as cane or steel replace the traditional whalebone stays.

Bodices could be plain or ornamented by a central plastron, which was varied by contrasting fabric, shirring, puckers, and horizontal or vertical tucks. Piping continued to outline many plastrons, and decorative buttons functional at one side frequently lined the edges so the

Slim-fitting polonaise has elegant plastron covered in part by lace fichu, three-quarter length sleeves, small outer watch pocket, and train descending straight to the floor before fanning. Peoria, Illinois.

there into points at either side. A border of satin usually edged the hem, with jet fringe or lace hanging below. Another variant, though much less popular and often left quite plain and un-adorned, opened at the waist, exposing a larger inverted V section of underskirt, which it ended only a few inches above.

Pointed or rounded apron fronts could also form the bottom of the polonaise. A single pointed apron could drape asymmetrically, but more often two were found crossing over one another. Sometimes the lower portion of the polonaise was hemmed straight and ac-cented by a series of horizontal folds or tucks, hugging the hips or extending below the knees. Occasionally the skirt attached diagonally to the bodice. Though emphasis was often placed at the hips, the overall look remained tightly sheathed.

The same variety of draperies displayed on the lower portion of the polonaise appeared on overskirts, which were worn with a separate bodice. Sometimes overskirts were dis-pensed with altogether, and it was on these skirts, or underskirts, where the real profusion of decorative elements prevailed. While bodices could range from elaborate to quite simple, the focus was from the waist down. There, a myriad of decorative stitches, which included tucks, horizontal folds, pleats, shirring, flounces (some fan-shaped), and more intermingled upon the skirt, providing quite a challenge to the dressmaker. A casu-ally draped swath of material that did not even seem an integral part of the costume proved equally difficult, as this interesting appendage could appear wrapped or "tied" anywhere about the skirt's circumfer-ence. Extra effort was not expended unnecessarily though, as underskirts were often left unadorned where covered by the bodice, polonaise, back drapery, or train. Such excess would have been unfeasible were it not for the sewing machine—and the inexpensive labor available to middle and upper classes in the form of outside laundresses or domes-tic servants, upon whose duty it fell to launder and iron the intricate garments.

To add even more complexity to outfits, the polonaise or bodice was often of a different fabric than the underskirt. Handsome materials abounded. Elegant velvets, brocades, and figured or watered silks were popular and could also be used for plastrons or to highlight portions of the skirt. (While luxurious fabrics were costly, the overall need for less material or their restriction to trim helped compensate.) One element that was not always present on the already overburdened garments was buttons, however, as back fastenings were becoming more com-monplace. Pockets too were apparently deemed excessive, and in spite

of the usefulness they would have afforded upon the narrow skirts, fashion decreed they again hide within the side seams.

Skirts were quite narrow and in the extreme hugged the body, descending straight from the hips to where inner ties held them so closely to the knees that steps were restricted. Skirts retained their elegant drapery in back, which began anywhere from the hips to the knees and formed an integral part of either the polonaise, skirt, or overskirt (which could be attached or a separate entity). Lavish drapery was less likely to flow into a lengthy train, however, as the popularity of that appendage was again diminishing. As if to accustom the public gradually to their inevitable demise, modest demi-trains that just brushed the floor were also used. While trains at first coexisted with shorter skirts (which cleared the ground by several inches), the wearing of the unwieldy extremities would, by the early eighties, be limited more often to carriage, evening, or at-home use. Their appear-ance would also change as longer trains rarely descended gradually but fell straight to the floor, where they formed a flat circular puddle. For added versatility, trains were avail-able in small detachable lengths that could be joined to the lower third of the dress when the occasion warranted. Though seldom utilized by women de-lighted to be rid of the troublesome article, modified bustles consisting of shallow half-

Long cuirass raised over hips and embellished by chiffon wrapped around throat and descending narrowly toward waist, intercepted by two large bows. Sandwich, Illinois.

springs or crinoline padding were an avail-able option to add a slight fullness from the waist down. Their usage would begin to increase during 1882, however, fore-shadowing the full-blown bustle that fash-ion authorities again deemed essential the following year.

Rounded cuirass with tucked, satin plastron partly hidden by long, narrow lace. Satin "tied" around hips; remainder of narrow skirt decorated with shirring and knife pleats. Mendota, Illinois.

Sleeves

The armscye began to move somewhat in from the point of the shoulder. Straight sleeves fit slightly loose and could extend to the wrist or bare a portion of the lower arm, as below-the-elbow lengths enjoyed a fleeting popularity. To complement the lace accents so prolific around the neck, turned-back cuffs were often featured in white linen or lace. Wide bands of white or black lace could also fall decoratively from below the sleeve, or it could be plain, tucked under in a simple hem. Occasionally, the shirring popularly used to accent portions of the garment enveloped the entire sleeve. The usual white under cuff or frill was generally absent from all but the decorative cuff edged with knife pleats, which retained its popularity from the late seventies.

Necklines

Necklines were still fairly high, with standing collars edged prominently underneath by a flaring white, pie-crust frill. Light- or dark-colored lace accents were especially fashionable. Fancy bows frequently ornamented the base of the collar, or lace might be pinned at or encircle the throat and lay bib-like upon the upper chest. Pieces of chiffon or lace could also wrap around the neck before descending narrowly to the waist, occasionally intercepted by bows. Cloth or lace "fichus" came in varied shapes, encircling the shoulders and covering substantial portions of the bodice. Small lace collars or larger, tubular-shaped entities were also available. A rare basque featured revers, and the space within, if not enclosed by cloth or a chemisette, was filled high to the neck with lace.

Jewelry

Brooches or bar pins often appeared pinned to the lace at the throat. Shorter sleeves left wrists exposed, encouraging display of the increasingly-favored bracelets. Wide gold, hand-engraved, black-enameled bangles, often displaying a "buckle" at the top, were especially popular—as were mesh bracelets with fancy slides and long "tails" hanging down the side. Thin, tubular-shaped bracelets featuring a cross over or wrap around section were also stylish. Watches, held by wide chains that most often hung sensibly around the neck, continued to repose in small (usually outer) pockets near the waist. Necklaces, generally with center extensions, remained quite popular, though earrings were worn less often and those seen were usually simple in design.

Hairstyles

The fashionable hairstyle was quite severe. Hair was pulled tightly back from the face and restricted in a low bun or a single braided loop. A flat bow often perched at the crown provided the sole height. Bangs, when worn, rendered the only softening to the face. They could be wispy, frizzed, or twisted into elaborate spit curls or loops painstakingly positioned upon the forehead and along the temples. While a center part was more common, hair could also be combed straight back from the face. In a rare moment of consciousness about the unflattering effect such styles might have upon broad faces or stubby necks, fashion decreed some height permissible. Many women were quick to take advantage of this leniency by retaining the more flattering rolls and chignons they had grown accustomed to wearing during the seventies.

Lots of shirring on skirt. Wide necklace with center extension sporting large locket; bar pin at throat. Hair pulled smooth and tight and crowned by large flat bow; bangs formed into tight, even curls. St. Louis, Missouri.

Polonaise forms panniers at hips that are outlined by satin and fringe. Flat bow at crown; deep, uniform curls on forehead. Garnett, Kansas.

Plain cuirass bodices with neck embellishments—all elaboration reserved for skirts. Altoona, Pennsylvania.

Cuirass with plastron over reverse, V-shaped overskirt. Long fringe highlights skirt. Very deep, white, pie-crust frill cradles neck. Mt. Pleasant, Iowa.

Plastron-enhanced cuirass forms W at hem. Typical lace at neck. Very straight, slim-fitting ensemble. Memphis, Missouri.

Simple but attractive polonaise, partially covered by large fichu, separates from bow into gentle, inverted V. Underskirt enhanced by a row of shirring above double pleated flounce. Central-parted hair pulled directly back and crowned by a flat white bow. Le Mars, Iowa.

Opposite Page

Deep cuirass with uniform hemline; lace at throat. Matching bracelets display long fancy slides and "tails." Hillsdale, Michigan.

Nora 707 BROADWAY, N.Y.

Pilgrimage outfit with pelerine; fancy parasol. New York, New York. (Possibly actress)

Diagonal-closing, inverted V-shaped polonaise or "casaque." Typical lace encircles neck and rests bib-like upon upper chest. Very severe hairstyle. Fergus Falls, Minnesota.

Revered cuirass forms W at hem. Highly shirred underskirt with accompanying long, puddling train. Hair formed into three vertical rolls and topped with hair comb. San Francisco, California.

Deep cuirass decorated with a yoke of heavy jet beads. Thick watch chain encircles neck; watch disappears within vertical slit of bodice. San Francisco, California.

Deep lace fichu covers most of cuirass (or polonaise)? Overskirt forms puffy panniers along hips. Underskirt heavily shirred—ends in three box-pleated flounces. Sacramento, California.

Opposite Page

Shallow pelerine over shirred and puckered plastron; reverse, V-shaped overskirt tops decorative underskirt. Veiled hat. Shelbyville, Illinois.

Fichu hides substantial portion of plain polonaise worn above decorative underskirt. Bangs formed into tight, precise curls; flat bow on crown. San Francisco, California.

Polonaise ends in prominent panniers. Three-quarter length sleeves have lace-edged, knife-pleated cuffs. Large horizontal rolls top head. Glasgow, Missouri. Hand dated "September, 1880."

Underskirt below deep, pointed, back-fastening cuirass shows casually "tied" fabric drape. Three-quarter sleeves are shirred—as is underskirt, which has decorative, fan-shaped flounces along hem. Napa, California.

Simple striped polonaise with large fichu worn over plain skirt. NM

Simple, inverted, V-shaped casaque worn over triple-flounced, box-pleated underskirt. Lace, turn-back cuffs; large fichu. Severe hairstyle. Chicago, Illinois.

Very elegant, probably dinner or trained carriage gown. Nantucket, Massachusetts. Card imprinted "1881." (Possibly actress)

Side view shows ensemble probably worn with modest bustle. Short basque bodice; three-quarter length sleeves end in a fall of black lace. Curled bangs along forehead and temple; large, flat bow on crown. Cleveland, Ohio.

Fancy studded beads highlight polonaise. Ornamental line of rosettes top double pleated flounce of underskirt. Stiff inner collar forms two points upon standing collar. NM

Long plain polonaise opens in reverse V and reaches near hem. Lace ties around neck and descends narrowly to waist. Fancy mesh bracelet with long tail and slide. San Francisco, California.

Figured velvet highlights ensemble. Revers filled by lace. Watch chain extends from central button hole; watch slides within vertical opening of bodice. Long train forms flat puddle on floor. Chicago, Illinois.

RIEMAN & CO.   26 Montgomery St.
Opposite Lick House.
Take Elevator.

Pilgrimage costume features deep cuirass ending in two shallow points. Trim on pelerine matches that on simple overskirt. San Francisco, California.

Duhem   2516 FOLSOM St. S.F.

Honeycombed plastron fronts deep, cord-draped and tasseled, slim-fitting polonaise. Collarette encircles standing collar, with inner, slightly-bent white standing band. Wide flat bow tops sleek hair with slight curling along temples. San Francisco, California.

Elegant fabric trims deep cuirass and underskirt. Horizontally-tucked plastron unbuttons at side. Sleeves retain triangular-shaped cuffs and double row of knife pleats popular during seventies. Braided chignon placed far back on crown and further ornamented by fancy comb. NM

Black lace falls from panniers and sleeves on polonaise and also heads deep knife pleats on underskirt. Hair forms tall chignon. Salem, Massachusetts.

Tubular-shaped lace collar with more lace pinned at throat tops decorative outfit. St. Joseph, Missouri. Hand dated "August, 1882."

Lots of shirring enhances the bodice of this belted polonaise. Aberdeen (state not identified).

Jet passementerie heavily encrusts elegant velvet cuirass and underskirt. Wide lace frill cradles neck. San Francisco, California.

Elegant brocaded polonaise. Philadelphia, Pennsylvania.

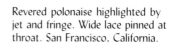

Revered polonaise highlighted by jet and fringe. Wide lace pinned at throat. San Francisco, California.

Short, diagonally-fastening brocade basque with velvet revers. Deep, pie-crust neck ruffle; lace attached at throat. Sacramento, California.

Black lace accents neckline of deeply-pointed basque. Fabric wraps around hip section of profusely shirred skirt, whose hem ends in pointed tabs over flounced accordion pleats. Watch hangs from thick chain around neck and disappears into small outside pocket near waist. Boonville, Missouri.

Overskirt attaches diagonally upon polonaise. Striped fabric used for plastron, triangular section of cuff, and pointed overskirt hem. Lace pinned to neck. Three rows of shirring top double box-pleated hem. Matching wide bangle bracelets. Stockton, California.

Elegant polonaise highlighted by shirring and beaded fringe. Mendota, Illinois.

116

Simple cuirass with turn-back lace cuffs and tubular-shaped, scalloped lace collar. Overskirt shaped in simple, inverted V ending in two points along the sides. Underskirt has double row of box pleats. Corset line visible beneath bodice. Large flat bow tops simple coiffure. Philadelphia, Pennsylvania.

Wedding photo. Buxom lady wears elaborate, bustled and trained gown. Merced, California.

Elegant brocaded fabric of basque highlights skirt. Dress shows re-emergence of bustle toward the end of the period. St. Louis, Missouri.

Chapter Fifteen

1883-1888

Woman seated at left wears rare belted basque colored differently from skirt and containing unusually large buttons. Lady seated to her right wears rare, full-flounced underskirt with unusually short bodice over simulated vest. Outfit of lady standing at right abounds in gaudily-swagged cords. Dayton, Ohio.

As the middle of the decade approached outfits again simplified, shedding the major portion of trim with which they were previously laden. Though bodices fit tightly, the hip encumbering cuirass was a thing of the past. Looser, gracefully draped skirts and fuller hairstyles lent a gentler, more relaxed air. The bustle reappeared in full force, but in a more angular form than that of the early seventies, and coupled with a scarcity of frills and ruffles the overall appearance, though softened, lacked the grace and femininity of its bustled predecessor. Instead stark outfits, snug bodices, and fuller skirts created a robust, buxom look that accentuated a large bosom and broad hips.

Outfits

The polonaise was almost entirely discarded in favor of the separate skirt, overskirt, and basque bodice. Overskirts continued to be supplied as integral or separate entities (known as "detachable draperies") and though simplified, still came in a variety of shapes. A new style featured two side panels that left the entire central area open to reveal the underskirt. Many favored an asymmetrical drape, the most popular taking the form of an overskirt first introduced in the early eighties. Sweeping diagonally across the front, it ended in a point near the hem or continued in an upward sweep toward the back. The standard, knee-length tablier periodically rose higher at one side and was especially stylish in a shallow version that hugged the hips or an elongated drape that culminated in a central "shawl point." A particularly intricate formation consisted of two lengths of fabric swaged asymmetrically across one another, though its relative complexity rendered it less desirable to the greater populace. Tabliers included upward-turning plaits along the side-back seams that imparted a handsomely cross-wrinkled appearance down their entire length. Sometimes one edge turned up "en revers" to expose the fabric beneath.

In stark contrast to the first few years of the eighties, underskirts were now quite plain. Skirts might employ gathers at the waist, resulting in loose vertical folds, but more often accordion, knife, or box pleats molded the entire surface or formed the hem of an otherwise plain skirt.

Skirts ended a couple inches from the floor and, while they hung fairly straight, they were fuller than the early eighties. Tie-backs still regulated skirts to the figure, but sufficient fabric allowed legs, newly liberated from their stringent tape enclosures, abundant freedom of movement. This was not always easy, however, as a preference for heavy woolen fabrics resulted in outfits that could weigh more than ten pounds (the increased weight on the waist and hips purported to assist the corset in displacing internal organs). Another obstacle existed in the bustle, which was revived from the early seventies to become the focal point of the costume—much to the dismay of women who believed themselves rid of the ponderous, backbreaking article. This version bore little resemblance to its predecessor, as it now formed a shelf-like construction that, in the extreme, jutted out at right angles, over which the overskirt abruptly fell to the floor. Trains were now exclusively relegated to evenings, their absence contributing to the less graceful appearance of the eighties daytime bustle. The fabric lying upon the full, half-length, or built-in tournure could have its

Dark velvet plastron and sleeves; simple, apron-shaped overskirt; pleated underskirt. Necklace with center extension. Curled hair at forehead and temples. Tipton, Missouri.

inserted as a permanent part of the outfit or made independently and in a variety of fabrics adaptable to several different costumes.

Bodices again buttoned exclusively in front, sometimes diagonally, and fit very smooth and tight, boned front and back with barely a crease evident. Corsets remained tightly laced to sustain the contrast of large hips and bosom with a tiny waist, and their outline was sometimes discernible beneath the skin-tight corsage. As snug bodices accentuated every curve, bust improvers were widely advertised to help those less endowed maintain the buxom look of the eighties. Sewing had to be more precise than ever with the stark, revealing garments, and tailor-finished costumes became quite fashionable, with every effort made in the cutting, seaming, lining, padding, and pressing to insure a perfect, wrinkle-free fit. By following the detailed instructions included in fashion magazines, the homemaker could achieve this finish with almost the same expertise as a professional tailor, and the exceptional fit lent an attractiveness to garments despite their austere appearance.

The now-scarce polonaise appeared principally in two styles that lingered from the early eighties—materializing the first two years in pannier-shaped designs and throughout the period in long plain dresses

drapery effect created by the simple application of single or multiple, downward-turning plaits along each side seam. At the center back, one or two "loopings and tackings" might be required. More intricate arrays continued to require attachment to tapes placed lengthwise (or crosswise) beneath the fabric. Some outfits lacked "bunched-up" drapery altogether, the material lying instead in smooth folds produced only from where it was pleated or gathered into the waistband. On rare occasions bouffant drapery sufficed without any superstructure, for a few garments were designed where bustles could be omitted if desired.

Basques usually extended only a few inches below the waist at the sides, with the below-the-hip length corsets used early in the decade receding accordingly. Though uniform hems existed, most formed a shallow curve or W in front or dipped to a shallow or, more frequently, very deep point. Occasionally longer lengths were preferred, with rounded hems extending to the hips. These (along with shorter versions) were sometimes called jerseys—a garment, like so many others in fashion, which changed considerably with the passage of time. Though still composed of more elastic materials, the typical jersey now resembled the standard bodice. Some basques exposed vests, which were more often simulated than real and attached flush with the bodice or inside along the darts or side seams. Postillions were a popular accompaniment, and in rare instances the rear portion of the basque bore the burden of attached lengths of long back drapery (described as a "basque front and polonaise back").

Bodices were most often plain, with no ornamentation except buttons, which, though not large, stood out prominently. A V neck or plastron sometimes interrupted the monotony of the surface. Filled with like or contrasting material (either smooth or enhanced by vertical tucks), they were periodically framed by revers, as piping was no longer stylish. While the fabric within most V necks buttoned up the center and formed an integral part of the bodice, a separate chemisette occasionally filled the void. In rare instances, bodices could feature a low-cut design or front closures that exposed part of the mid-section, and these too were filled with chemisettes (often in vertically pleated versions known as "plaited vests"). These versatile articles were either

Deep, asymmetrically-draped overskirt surmounts pleated underskirt. Figured velvet revers, collar, and cuffs. Necklace with center extension and bar pin at collar. Scranton, Kansas.

opening into an inverted V upon the skirt. The redingote overdress appeared with even less frequency and its form, in common with the jersey, had also evolved. One version resembled a floor length coat left open down the front. Another, more common variant, was but a continuation of the bodice and featured fabric contained within the armscye, shoulder, and neck seams that fell loosely open upon the skirt below.

An occasional over- or underskirt consisted of different-colored fabric from the bodice, but most matched (with darker shades preferred, though white was popular during the summer). Contrasting materials in like shades became increasingly popular, however, providing texture and variety to outfits otherwise almost devoid of decorative trim. Satin and velvet, which now appeared figured, checked, and striped as well as plain, were especially favored. Decorative fabric found on the skirt, most commonly as a rectangular strip down one side of the underskirt, usually complemented the bodice, forming collars, cuffs, revers, or plastrons. On rare occasions bodice accents were asymmetrically placed, with one side bearing absolutely no relation to the other. While most outfits lacked applied trim, thick cord and fancy, beaded or braided passementerie proved the exception on a few. Jet beads could be tastefully applied or amassed in great profusion, adding considerably to the garment's overall weight. Thick cords might appear gaudily swaged down the entire length of the ensemble.

Sleeves

Skin tight sleeves were now in vogue, making arm movements difficult and forcing women to literally "peel off" their bodices (though more practical-minded women often indulged in sleeves having some "give"). On rare occasions the top portion provided some ease, though the raised fabric did not approach the height characteristic of sleeves from the next time period. While three-quarter lengths were available, long sleeves typically ended just short of the wrist. Square cuffs of velvet or satin often complemented other trim. Sleeves might also be perfectly plain, devoid of cuffs and merely turned under in a simple hem, sometimes decorated with jet beads or braid. Although not universal, a plain white band or, less often, frill basted underneath returned to favor.

Necklines

While an occasional turn-down collar was utilized, stiff, moderately-high standing collars were the norm, often of satin or velvet to match other trim. Just visible underneath was an equally stiff standing collar band. Though these could still be basted to the inside, they were generally attached to a shallow dickey. Inner bands overlapped where they fastened at the front, and a vertical

Figured velvet highlights skirt and bodice. White, pie-crust frill at neck. Face softly framed by short curls. Matching bangle bracelets. North Anson, Maine.

Simple skirt, basque, and long, asymmetrically-draped overskirt. Washington, Pennsylvania.

Beaded passementerie ornaments bodice and sleeves. Short, apron-shaped tablier over knife-pleated underskirt. York, Nebraska.

striped pattern sometimes varied the standard white. Less frequently, a modest, pie-crust frill in either white or black lace presented a gentler ornament around the neck. Decorative jabots appeared but rarely to soften the austere appearance, though an occasional "dog collar" formed of jet, often with dangling pendants, could be fastened about the throat. Scarce, detachable plastrons composed entirely of beads might also beautify a plain bodice. An unusual fad featuring a handkerchief casually tucked beneath the first few buttons of the corsage or peering out from under the basque periodically relieved the severity of the ensemble.

Jewelry

The overall look was crisp, neat, and uncluttered. Little jewelry was indulged except the ubiquitous bar pin, which had the practical purpose of holding the two sections of collar together at the throat. As if to add some levity to stark outfits, these were offered in novelty designs featuring animals, birds, insects, horseshoes, and Japanese fans—along with the standard engraved pins. Watch chains were conspicuously absent around the neck. Though long chains were still used, they again dangled, as in the sixties, from a button hole of the basque or looped from there over the bar pin, and short chains featuring decorative fobs were just becoming fashionable. A few outer pockets lingered above the waist, but watches were most often secreted within a small pocket above the bosom, just inside the central opening—making retrieval awkward, as it must certainly involve unfastening at least one button of the corsage. Necklaces were used sparingly and formed primarily of box links or narrow mesh supporting center extensions (though a few featured their small lockets directly attached). Taille d' epergne bangles (still featured in sets) and bracelets that overlapped in front remained stylish. Ears were either bare or graced by a small ball or other simple ornament hanging just below the lobe, and earrings were no longer designed to match the brooch.

Hairstyles

Bangs reached the height of their popularity and became the focal point of the hairstyle. No longer restricted to the forehead, they were often cut in a swath from ear to ear, creating a gentle arch about the face. Separated into a large section at the top of the head, frequently with smaller portions included along the temples, hair was cut short and either frizzed or softly curled and worn partially down upon the forehead, the greater portion adding height at the top and sides, or, more rarely, combed into very straight bangs. The remaining hair was typically drawn into a bun positioned where it would just be visible at the top of the head. Sometimes a large horizontal roll appeared sandwiched between the bun and fringe. This periodically formed the support (or a separate cushion was added) for bangs that, instead of being worn down, were combed back off the forehead, as became popular toward the end of the period. Occasionally a few short, curly locks lay gently upon the neck to help soften the appearance.

Left:

Revers and tucked V neck contrast with velvet bodice. Knife-pleated side panels surround velvet overskirt. San Francisco, California. Hand dated "1885."

Right:

Less-favored, turn-down collar on beautiful striped bodice. Deep central shawl point of overskirt falls upon plain underskirt decorated with three narrow, box-pleated flounces. Sacramento, California.

Checked bodice highlighted with velvet at collar, cuffs, and outer watch pocket. Skirt has long asymmetrical drape with velvet strip along one side. Peoria, Illinois.

Unusual velvet trim woven through box pleats of underskirt coordinates beautifully with bodice. Brookfield, Missouri.

H. J. Corell,   ELDRED, PA.

Simple ensemble laden with beaded passementerie. Eldred, Pennsylvania.

Stanton & Burdick,   119-129 NORTH MAIN ST., LOS ANGELES, CAL.

Simple bodice decorated with vertical rows of braided passementerie. (Note interesting placement of watch within trim.) Los Angeles, California.

Rare bodice features cutout at chest, attached overskirt panels, and three-quarter length sleeves. Marysville, California.

Elite Gallery, Griffiths Marysville, Cal.

Rare bodice is open at chest and filled probably by separate chemisette. One-sided, draped overskirt; underskirt with narrow, box-pleated hem. Eldred, Pennsylvania.

C. B. Colburn, BAY CITY, MICH.

Beautiful figured-velvet bodice and underskirt. Overskirt forms central shawl point. Watch chain loops around bar pin; watch tucked inside bodice revers above what is possibly a chemisette. Bay City, Michigan.

Plaid revers, collar, cuffs, and skirt trim coordinate beautifully with outfit. Revers surround simulated vest. Sacramento, California.

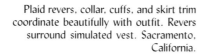

ASHER 810 J Street SACRAMENTO, CAL.

Side view displays modest bustle; pointed basque; short, apron-shaped overskirt; box-pleated underskirt. NM

Ultra-simple yet perfectly fitted and attractive ensemble. (Note vertical stripes on inner collar band.) Hair curled at temples, forehead, and behind neck. Sacramento, California.

Apron-shaped overskirt with large bustle surmounts box-pleated underskirt. Necklace features center extension. Bethany, Missouri.

Diagonal bodice closure featured with asymmetrically-draped overskirt. Joliet, Illinois.

Sleek, perfect-fitting bodice and large, bustled overskirt. Hair curled along forehead, temples, and top of head. NM

Elegant bustled ensemble features open area above shirred plastron possibly filled by chemisette; Victoria watch chain depends from gap. Los Angeles, California.

Side view shows extreme horizontal bustle. Zanesville, Ohio.

221 N. MAIN STREET,
(Downey Block.)
LOS ANGELES, - - - CAL.

Lawrence & Son.

Beads fashioned into "rain" decorate sleek ensemble. Large, horizontal bustle. Los Angeles, California

White summertime outfit with three-quarter length sleeves. Wrap-around bracelet. NM

Henry,   Abbott   Illinois.

Buxom lady wears rare stripped polonaise with large buttons and turn-down collar. Henry, Illinois.

Corsage of lady standing features turn-down collar, three-quarter length sleeves, and tucks at upper chest that probably close with hidden hooks and eyes above prominent buttons of lower bodice. Seated lady wears rare polonaise; large locket hangs directly from simple chain. Marysville, California.

Scarce redingote descends halfway upon underskirt. Chicago, Illinois.

M. E. PHARES,   Oroville, Cal.

No. 171 Main Street, Oshkosh

Both ladies' bodices are skin tight. Bodice at right incorporates simulated vest; horseshoe-shaped brooch replaces usual bar pin on collar; watch secreted between bodice buttons, probably in special pocket. Oroville, California.

Outfit at left features velvet collar, plastron, and cuffs. A horizontal roll is clearly visible in each lady's hairdo. Oshkosh, Wisconsin.

Bodice buttons at the side of figured plastron. Watch fits between buttons, probably in special pocket. Two knife-pleated panels surround figured velvet underskirt. Jamestown, New York.

Bodice features asymmetrical design; skirt has knife pleated side panels. Riverside, California.

Chapter Sixteen

1889-1892

Sleeves were the distinctive feature of the entire decade, most costumes being datable by viewing the upper portion alone. The slim, peaked sleeves and straight, narrow skirts returned a vertical emphasis to the early nineties. The long reign of the overskirt, popular for the past two decades, ceased. Bustles, too, retreated into obscurity. Simple skirts, lacking imaginative over-drapery or other ornamentation, diverted attention to the variety of decorative innovations embodied upon the bodice (though the first few years of the decade would remain subdued in contrast with what would follow).

Lady seated far right wears jacket to match skirt, with double-pointed Swiss "girdle" (with matching collar) worn over blouse. Plastron of lady standing to her left encloses draped fabric formed by pleats along the shoulder seams. Two of the ladies wear simple chain and locket chokers. NM

Outfits

Basques remained fully boned and tight. Most extended one to several inches at the sides and back, giving them a long-waisted appearance as they dipped slightly at center front to a point or shallow curve. Occasionally they spread in uniform depth to mid-hip. Bodice fabric continued to match the skirt, and though solid colors predominated—still occasionally accented with velvet (generally un-figured) or satin—plaids periodically offered a welcome relief. Except for sleeves, many bodices bore a strong resemblance to those that, during the eighties, had featured V necks or plastrons, as these features were now used extensively. Options within plastrons expanded to include like or contrasting fabric that could be smooth, puckered, lined with

from the center and attaching it along the left side. Revers or trim applied only to one side frequently heightened the asymmetrical appeal of diagonal closures. Though used sparingly, when trim appeared on the bodice (popularly in fancy passementerie or narrow strips of ribbon or gimp), it was generally repeated on the cuffs, collar, and skirt bottom.

Most bodices had ornamentation concentrated on the upper chest in designs that narrowed upon approaching the waist. Decoration could begin with shirring, followed by progressively constricting pleats. Some were fashioned from fabric arranged in folds at one or both shoulders that thinned during its downward sweep toward the opposite side. The triangular-shaped plastrons and V necks by definition broadened the chest as they "pointed" toward the mid-section. Accentuated further by full upper sleeves, pointed bodices, and horizontal skirt

Striped bodice contains long hip flaps and sleeves only slightly raised at shoulders. Revers frame vertically-tucked plastron. Plain skirt. Hair curled on top, smooth and tight above ears. Stockton, California.

Lace trim frames plastron. Skirt pleated at sides, draped in center. Philadelphia, Pennsylvania.

vertical tucks, or given a draped effect by the inclusion of pleats along the shoulder seams. Both plastrons and V necks were often edged by revers or a narrow row of gimp. A chemisette generally filled the gap within V-shaped necklines and could be attached permanently to one side or worn as a separate entity, with ties still included at the waist holding it secure. Fancy postillions disappeared along with the bustle, though separate appendages of like or contrasting material were sometimes sewn about the waist, extending as flaps in varying lengths upon the hips. While center, off-center, or diagonal closures were the norm, the mid-section could also be uninterrupted by buttons or hidden hooks and eyes; these were used to fasten the bodice at the left side, above the shoulder and beneath the arm, and invisibly at the center front of an inner lining, carrying the outer fabric of the bodice over

trim, all were geared to create the illusion of a tiny waist, made smaller in actuality by the time-honored corset. Despite the now-abundant medical evidence regarding the benefits of exercise and freedom of movement, the wasp waist remained a much-desired objective, with the fashionable woman reluctant as ever to relinquish her body-molding stays.

The skirt and shirtwaist reappeared occasionally for street wear, though a few more years would pass before they achieved complete acceptance. While sufficient unto themselves, they were most often coordinated with jackets, as the "tailor-made" assumed the familiar form of shirt, coat, and skirt. Jackets could be long or short, were often worn open to expose a vest or shirt, and in rare instances contained moderate to floor-length coat tails. Blouses too became available. Resembling shirtwaists but made without a waistband, they extended to the hips and were equally stylish when worn outside the skirt. Belts graced the waist and often dipped at center front, where they might overlap or form double points reminiscent of the Swiss versions common during the sixties (known now as "girdles" and sometimes sporting suspenders). Jackets sometimes accompanied the standard bodice and skirt.

Overskirts were no longer fashionable with the exception of the rare "Russian" outfit, a fad popular in 1892 featuring a simple, knee-length overskirt shaped identically to the underskirt. The overskirt could also consist of a knee-length, belted blouse or polonaise. It was also during this time that the princess dress reappeared, though neither outfit achieved much notice. The standard bodice continued to be far more popular, occasionally appearing as a "Marguerite basque," which displayed gathered contrasting fabric contained within a wide yoke, the smooth portion beneath occasionally split down the center to the waist.

Skirts were just slightly gored in front, with darts producing a snug fit at the stomach and hips, where they descended in an almost straight line to the floor. Some presented a plain, smooth surface, while others possessed shallow drapes of fabric created by inward-turning plaits along the waist. Occasionally, fabric was fashioned into knife or box pleats carefully pressed to fall from the waistband in narrow folds. Sometimes only the sides were pleated, with the center falling smooth or with a slight drape. Ornamentation was seldom used and found generally at the hem in a band of ruffles, pleats, or contrasting fabric. Contrasting fabric also lingered from the eighties in a decorative, one-sided vertical strip. Though bustles had, for the most part, disappeared, modified "pads" or springs were still available to add a slight fullness beneath the gathered or pleated folds of fabric, which fell from the waist in a simple "waterfall" effect held neatly in place underneath by a horizontally-placed tape or elastic band.

A subtle change began to take place in skirt design by 1892. Still hanging straight at the sides, skirts presented an unblemished surface interrupted only by the occasional horizontal trim, periodically placed knee-length to simulate a Russian over blouse. They could be constructed either from modest gores or the newer fan shape, which consisted of a rectangular front breadth joined to a semicircular breadth in back or of a single, fan-shaped section of fabric that met in a solitary back seam. Aided by darts, all fit smoothly around the torso, sweeping the bulk of the fabric backward to meet most commonly in

Simple plaid ensemble: bodice has turn-down collar and moderate hip flaps. San Francisco, California.

Bodice forms V neck, probably filled by separate chemisette. Skirt carefully knife pleated at sides, with horizontal trim near hem. Milton, North Dakota.

inverted pleats. Despite repeated assurances about the permanence of walking skirts, the deep folds thus created expanded outward upon the floor, resulting in a brief revival of the demi-train for daytime apparel.

Sleeves

Sleeves were usually tight half to three-quarters of the distance up the arm. The upper portion was always raised, most often looking as if the slight looseness of gathered fabric had been pushed in on the sides, forcing it to kick-up above the shoulder line—often to the extreme of angling inward. Crescent-shaped pads attached to the lining supplied the necessary support. The heightened fabric forced the armscye further inside, where it assumed a vertical stance between the arm and shoulder joint. This narrow shoulder span imparted a timid aspect to the wearer that contrasted sharply with the confident air soon to be conveyed by the broad-shouldered outfits of mid-decade.

Three sleeve types were worn besides the standard article, though with much less frequency. While different in appearance, all shared the distinctive peak at the shoulder. The bishop, still favored on shirtwaists, fell with equal fullness from armscye to cuff. Another style hung full and limp from shoulder to elbow, with tight sleeves below. A variant—which did not appear until about 1892—though similar in aspect, was actually a double sleeve, with the upper sleeve ending at the elbow.

Sleeves were long, stopping at or just above the wrist. They could feature triangular-shaped, turned-back cuffs that flared slightly or could end in a simple hem, which was sometimes embellished with a row of the same trim used elsewhere upon the garment. Separate fabric rarely edged the sleeves underneath.

Necklines

Necklines displayed greater diversity. Along with the advent of side-fastening bodices, high standing collars could now wrap entirely about the neck. Small, turn-down collars might hug the nape while angling downward toward the throat, surrounding it with a V shape. Or, they could appear flush with the bodice, meeting at center front in points or gentle curves. Sometimes collars were omitted. In their place, the fabric of plastrons, chemisettes, or bodices was simply rounded and sewn close along the edge to form a tiny ruffle. When present, collars and revers could be the same fabric as the bodice or coordinate with other trim. In keeping with cuffs, the separate white collar band or frill worn beneath was no longer requisite, though it remained popular for higher necklines.

Jewelry

With the exception of the still-popular bar pin, which increasingly performed a solely decorative function at the base of the throat, jewelry seldom enlivened the rather somber appearance of the costumes. Though wrists were often visible, bracelets—generally fashioned from thin wire and sold singly—were scarce. Necklaces too were unfashionable. At most, chokers made from beads or a small locket and chain graced throats left bare in the absence of high collars. Watch chains, if used at all, were of the shorter variety. Called "Victorias," they resembled those long used by men and generally hung from a front button, the watches themselves secreted alongside the central opening. Sometimes, the smaller chains and fob dangled over the edge of bodices featuring a separate fabric at the chest, with the watch then caught beneath in a small pocket attached to the bodice lining. Ears remained bare or accented by simple, suspended ornaments.

Bodice plastron framed by knife pleats, which continue down skirt. Turn-down collar fits high on neck and angles downward toward throat. Redwood Falls, Minnesota.

Simple plaid ensemble decorated with velvet plastron, cuffs, and horizontal skirt trim. Sioux Falls, South Dakota.

Hairstyles

At first glance hairstyles greatly resembled the previous period. A large section of hair at the top of the head was still cut into a curly fringe; however, the hair about the temples was frequently swept tightly back from the face, making the ears prominent and giving the overall appearance of a wide, curly Mohawk. A very short, thin row of bangs was combed down over the forehead, the remainder being curled upward to add height. Buns lowered to the hairline and were not visible from the front.

Interesting bar pin in the shape of a key decorates standing collar. Skirt features simple box pleats. NM

Sleeves kick high above shoulder. Bodice has standing velvet collar with inner, pie-crust frill and tapered plaid plastron framed by velvet revers. A plaid strip marks one side of the skirt, which is pleated into the waistband to give a slight drape. San Francisco, California.

Bodice closes asymmetrically. Inner chemisette or filler sewn near edge to form small neck ruffle. Watch disappears beneath bodice opening, leaving only small Victoria chain visible. San Francisco, California.

Sleeves have severe kick up, angling armscye inward and making wearer look rather timid. Fancy gimp outlines bodice and plastron. Bar pin accents base of turn-down collar. Sioux City, Iowa.

Wedding photo. Tucked and puckered plastron surrounded by fancy gimp. Pleats at waist produce slight drape down skirt front. San Francisco, California.

Simple ensemble with standing collar, peaked sleeves, and plastron. Hair curled on top and forehead, sleek above ears. Sioux City, Iowa.

Left:

Raised sleeves; narrow puckered plastron; low rounded collar. Corset line is visible beneath bodice. Interesting narrow ribbon flaps decorate top of skirt. Santa Rosa, California.

Right:

Wedding photo. Long, hiplength bodice; puckered, triangular-shaped plastron framed by gimp sports low ruffled collar; triangular-shaped, turn-back flaring cuffs; simple skirt. New York, New York.

Left:

Long, hiplength bodice; puckered, triangular-shaped plastron framed by gimp with low ruffled collar; triangular-shaped, turn-back flaring cuffs; simple skirt. New York, New York.

Right:

Wedding photo. Narrow strips of velvet ribbon decorate bodice and skirt. Chicago, Illinois.

G. G. Kimball,   COUDERSPORT, PA.

Kick-up sleeves; standing collar; puckered plastron framed by gimp; two simple flounces at skirt hem. Coudersport, Pennsylvania.

Young lady wears loose-fitting jacket over simple, side-fastening bodice. Horizontal rows of skirt trim matched on bodice and jacket. Cambridge, Minnesota.

Bodice has pleats along one shoulder forming asymmetrical drape; box pleated skirt. (Note tiny waistline!) NM Hand dated "April, 1891."

Seated lady wears open jacket sporting long coat tails over what appears to be a separate blouse and vest. Striped outfit features diagonal closure with one-sided rever; sleeves raised and full to elbow, tight-fitting below. Watsonville, California.

Lady seated far right wears version of Marguerite basque, split down center front. Blouse of lady seated far left rests outside skirt, has interesting puffed sleeves. Dixon, Illinois. Photo dated "January, 1892."

Top Left:

Bodice closes side front, has turn-down collar and double sleeve. Omaha, Nebraska.

Center Left:

Wedding photo. Peaked oversleeves reach elbow length, with tight-fitting sleeves below. Ft. Wayne, Indiana.

Bottom Left:

Seated lady displays Marguerite basque: wide gathered yoke above smooth-fitting waist. Wide horizontal band of velvet accents skirt hem. San Francisco, California.

Simple bodice closes with hidden hooks and eyes. Overskirt possibly a later addition to "update" ensemble into newer "Russian" look. Corvallis, Oregon.

Ladies in back row wear V necks filled most likely by chemisettes, sewn in tiny ruffles around neck. Lady on right has separate oversleeves; watch tucked above chemisette, Victoria chain hanging outside. Bodices of seated ladies feature shirred yokes. Cedar Rapids, Iowa.

Ladies Russian outfit: long belted polonaise over matching skirt. Kingman, Kansas.

Raised shoulders; diagonal closure; belt dips center waist; bodice opening filled with lace; skirt fullness drawn into train. Beaded choker worn around neck. Manchester, New Hampshire.

Ruffles and gathers on chest lead down to central pointed waist; sleeves full above elbow; ruffled skirt hem. Hair curled on top, sleek above ears. San Francisco, California.

Shirring above chest tapers to slim-fitting bodice. Skirt trimmed midway to simulate Russian overskirt; fullness taken to back, resulting in shallow train. Oakland, California.

1893-1896

The mid-nineties was an era of both exaggeration and contrast. In clothing, everything was done in a "big way." Such elements as revers, lapels, collars, cuffs, and especially sleeves, were not just big, they could be enormous! Tiny, tightly-corseted waists contrasted with flaring skirts and top-heavy torsos to create what was then referred to as the "hourglass figure." Tight, close hairstyles appeared disproportionate with the flamboyant garments, and all combined to give women a comic, almost doll-like appearance.

Outfits

After a twenty-seven-year reign the basque gave way to a bodice that once again ended at the waistline, though an occasional jacket-style bodice incorporating a smooth or flaring basque (called a "circular peplum") was recommended for those who did not find a round waist especially becoming. Bodices covered the waistband of the skirt, sometimes dipping just enough at the sides and front to lend a long-waisted appearance, and were held firm upon the back of the skirt with hooks and eyes. Round waists favored "belts," which were characteristically simulated by darker- or lighter-colored material. Visible or hidden center, off-center, and side closures continued to offer greater options to vary the look of the corsage. Outfits of a single, solid-colored fabric still prevailed, and jet and lace reemerged as fashionable bodice trim. Contrasts were occasionally provided by the ever-popular velvet or satin fabrics confined within straight or square yokes or upon collars, cuffs, and revers.

Bodices came in many different styles. Some were fully boned, fitting smooth and snug. Others displayed full gathers beneath a wide yoke. (While appearing more comfortable, fabric was usually loosely mounted above a tightly-fitting, boned inner lining.) Some fit smooth and tight around the mid-section with fulled pleats below the neck. To achieve this, fabric and lining united below the bosom, closing invisibly with hooks and eyes; above, pleated fabric separated from the lining (which continued its hook and eye closure to the neck), remaining open in the center and often providing access and a convenient resting place for a small watch. Many bodices featured loose fabric at center front formed by gathers along the neck and waist (often incorporated within a plastron). By 1895, this looseness developed into a fuller "French-" or "blouse front" that actually sagged upon the waistband below. A large central box pleat could also achieve this drooping effect, as could a separate chemisette-like garment made of silk, lace,

Bodice of lady standing at left features separate oversleeves looped up at the sides. Seated lady has large, leg-of-mutton sleeves; velvet yoke; thin watch chain around neck, with watch disappearing within side-front opening. Both ladies' hairstyles feature top knots. Astoria, Oregon.

Blouses were most often white (though colors were available) and either plain or decorated with pinstripes, polka dots, or checks. Dressier styles were difficult to distinguish from bodices and could be open in the center, displaying a fancy front, or enhanced with narrow, simulated bolero vest flaps. Bolero vests, which had reappeared early in the nineties, could also be donned separately. In common with looser-appearing bodices, shirts and blouses were mounted upon close linings that belied their more casual appearance.

Early ensemble featuring full sleeves above the elbow and the horizontal skirt trim fashionable in 1892 and 1893. Los Angeles, California.

Shirts were frequently accompanied by myriad jackets: casual blazers; stylish "Etons" with their ample lapels; and numerous other short or long, single or double-breasted styles. As tailored suits were worn year round, full sleeveless "vests" were recommended beneath for warm weather. Assuming a new look virtually indistinguishable from a blouse, vests could fasten at the front, side, or back and provided a far cooler and less bulky summertime option. Both tailored suits and the skirt and blouse were considered especially appropriate for single women beginning to move away from traditional occupations such as laundresses, domestics, or dressmakers. Since either could be varied with a simple change of shirt or neck dressing, they were both affordable and stylish and felt more in keeping with the professional look required of clerical workers or department store clerks. Such mix and match ensembles afforded everyone the appearance of an expanded wardrobe without the expense.

As sleeves expanded skirts became progressively wider to help balance the upper torso. Using gores alone (numbering anywhere from four to nine) or the many variations of the newer fan shape—rather than relying upon pleats for constriction, which had been the case the last time skirts reached such widths in the sixties—resulted in a smooth, snug fit about the hips. This required tightly-laced corsets to achieve the desired hourglass effect, which accentuated broad hips as well as a tiny waist. Encompassing hip

Skirts become more triangular shaped. Bodice is waist length with large epaulets. Skirt features horizontal skirt trim still popular during 1893. Los Angeles, California.

or chiffon known as a "front." This might supply the mid-section for bodices left open at the center and was periodically placed directly on top of bodices, completely altering their appearance.

Though outlandish enough in their own right, garments were often far simpler than those illustrated in fashion plates, whose depictions had become especially exuberant. French plates showed plastrons in fantastic shapes and sizes while in actuality, most assumed a simple rectangular or triangular form. Even American drawings featured detachable pointed peplums, elaborate trim, and overlarge skirts sporting recurrent overskirts that rarely appeared upon the more subdued garments adopted by the general public. While seldom as dramatic as depicted, revers on bodices (frequently square shaped) and jackets could reach exceptional proportions. This was also true of "bretelles," which resembled revers but were applied as a decorative trim that flared out over the shoulders before tapering to a point front and back. When properly lined to hold their shape and used in combination with large collars, cuffs, and sleeves, the effect was not only impressive but quite effective at enhancing the broad-shouldered, narrow-waisted appearance.

The blouse or shirtwaist was now widely embraced for both the street and home, achieving a popularity that far eclipsed what it had known in the sixties and enjoyed by young and old alike. While "waists" were still pictured with several inches of material showing beneath a belt, they were usually neatly tucked inside the waistband, which was then covered by a fabric belt featuring a large, ornate silver buckle.

pads could even be purchased for further emphasis. Skirts flared from the waist into the shape of a triangle—and as the hoop, while threatened, was never revived—the greater circumference at the hem, coupled with insufficient support, caused them to fall in broad "umbrella folds." Though never attaining the size illustrated in fashion magazines, sufficient foundation was achieved by muslin petticoats gored to flare at the bottom and ending in a deep flounce, which could rest upon narrow, gathered ruffles or be stiffened with stitched cords. While the front of the skirt often hung with only slight undulations, gathers or box pleats behind the waist produced fabric that radiated outward, culminating in pronounced folds or "godets." Much effort was expended to enable these to maintain their shape without appearing stiff and inflexible. One rather drastic solution called the "La Pliante" featured pliable bands of steel that fit in upper and lower rows beneath the fabric of the skirt or petticoat. Straps were attached at intervals that, when buckled, caused the bands to curve outward, literally forcing the overlying material into the required shape. The search for suitable underlinings (such as hair cloth or "fibre chamois") proved far more practical, however. These, aided by an elastic strap tacked beneath the godets, usually proved sufficient and were equally beneficial in molding the less pronounced "flutes" constituting the remainder of the skirt.

Skirts were distinctive at this time by their noticeable lack of ornamentation (except for 1893, when horizontal trim remained in vogue) and now fell unblemished from waist to hem. They were fuller in back, but trains were again out of fashion except for evening wear. Skirt lengths varied throughout the nineties and could just brush the floor or be an inch or two removed. Hems continued to receive protection against fraying from a balayeuse or from velvet or braided hem protectors.

Sleeves

The voluminous sleeves were the focal point of the garment, not reaching such proportions since their inception in the 1830s. Though eventually extreme to the point of absurdity, the resulting broad-shouldered effect nevertheless imparted a robust, confident air to the wearer, reflecting well the woman newly "liberated" into the fields of sports and business. The "balloon" or "puffed" sleeve's fullness ended abruptly above the elbow, where it then fit snug to the wrist. Though closely resembling each other, in the more popular "leg-of-mutton" (or "gigot"), the upper fullness tapered more gradually to the tightly-fitting lower portion. Both became progressively larger, and a miniature wire hoop was even patented in 1896 to prevent the collapse of sleeves that by

then had grown especially massive. Stiff inner linings were generally adequate, however, and often fit snug around the upper arm, obviating any relief the loose outer portion may have provided. In an interesting variation of the balloon style, a full oversleeve separated or looped up at the side, exposing a triangular portion of the separate, fitted undersleeve. In addition to the styles currently in fashion, bishop sleeves, albeit fuller, remained an option for blouses. Epaulets formed from sizable flaps of fabric or lace periodically intensified the broadening impact of the sleeves.

Though often ending with a simple hem and no other decoration, deep, scalloped and flared, turned-back "mousquetaire" cuffs often provided a pleasing balance to the top-heavy sleeve. The separate under cuffs that had been popular for so long were finally discarded, though the cuffs themselves were often detachable.

Necklines

Standing collars were worn quite high on the neck and generally fastened at the side or back (though an occasional collar turned down upon the neck or flush with the bodice). In common with cuffs, detachable versions were available, and inner collar bands ceased to be worn. When upright, wire-strengthened fans of lace were featured becomingly framing the face from behind, the collar was referred to as a "Medici" or "Valois." Appropriately named for their slightly mashed look, "crush" collars featured horizontal folds and were often accompanied by large bows at the back. (Though appearing more malleable, these were fashioned over stiff inner collar bands.) Some outfits contained an additional cape-like collar or "bertha," worn flat, fluted, or featuring Vandykes, which could reach exceptionally wide proportions as it extended over the shoulders and bosom. This could be perma-

Full pleats below neck rest loosely above a centrally-closed inner lining, allowing access for a watch, whose small Victoria chain is left exposed. Balloon sleeves; matching figured trim on belt, collar, and wide bertha. Chicago, Illinois.

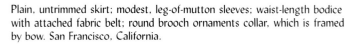

Plain, untrimmed skirt; modest, leg-of-mutton sleeves; waist-length bodice with attached fabric belt; round brooch ornaments collar, which is framed by bow. San Francisco, California.

Two large hair combs help flatten hair at either side of central part. Small, heart-shaped locket attaches to simple chain. Benson, Minnesota.

Bodice of lady on the left features side closure, gathered fabric between yoke and pointed fabric "belt," and high standing collar. Bodice of companion closes side front. West Superior, Wisconsin.

nently affixed or available as one of the many detachable options especially popular to alter or enhance the costume. Separate lace collarettes, which often incorporated a yoke and were rounded, squared, T, or V shaped, covered such sizable portions of the shoulders and chest that besides enriching an outfit, they were recommended as a cover-up for half-worn bodices. So too were the frilly bretelles and plastrons anchored by wide crushed belts or pointed girdles. Velvet revers or jet fashioned into "rain" or other decorative designs could also be applied. Blouses and tailored suits frequently sported masculine neck- or, less often, bow ties, or an occasional frilly jabot cascaded upon the bosom to lend a more elegant touch.

Jewelry

Silver began to vie with gold as a popular jewelry medium, though little of either was worn during the day to compete with the flamboyant garments. Thin watch chains reappeared occasionally about the neck, often materializing in a narrow black braid with slide that had been popular during the eighteen-forties and fifties. The shirtwaist and skirt returned the belt to favor, and watches were again tucked beneath, sometimes attached to the shorter Victoria chains that draped casually over the side. Though just becoming available in stores, the small open-faced watches called "chatelaines," which hung from a pin at the breast, would not enjoy significant favor until the first decade

of the new century. Bar pins were frequently displaced by a small round brooch of twisted gold or a horizontally-placed stick pin. Ears were left bare except for an occasional appearance of the recently-invented studs. Thin necklaces with small round, square, or, more popularly, heart-shaped lockets directly attached, and the chain and heart-shaped padlock bracelet enjoyed widespread popularity—but were reserved mostly for evening wear.

Hairstyles

Conservative coiffures tempered flamboyant costumes. While the full, bouffant "pompadour" worn the first decade of the twentieth century would have seemed more appropriate to balance the figure, women's hairstyles were instead worn fairly tight and close to the head, thus diverting even more attention to their cumbersome apparel. A thin row of short, tightly-curled bangs was usually present, behind which hair was either parted in the center or combed straight back into a distinctive topknot. At times the topknot was excluded, replaced perhaps by a fancy silver or tortoise shell comb. When bangs were not present, a central part preceded hair lightly waved (though not adding any significant breadth), with ears left bare or only partially covered and possibly one or two spit curls upon the forehead. Special "bang" combs were common at either side of the part to help the loose ends of hair, which had recently added height to eighties and early nineties coiffures, conform to the current, flatter styles.

Bodice fits smooth along mid-section, with loose pleats above, and is accented by dark velvet collar, "belt," and square revers. Pemberville, Ohio.

Drooping center of fancy striped shirtwaist might be an integral plastron or separate, chemisette-like front. Triangular-shaped, flared, mousquetaire cuffs. Providence, Rhode Island.

Tight, side-fastening bodice displays beaded jet yoke and large, leg-of-mutton sleeves. Hair has short curled bangs and tall hair comb. Manchester, New Hampshire.

Wedding photo. Full, side-closing bodice set on snug, central-hooking inner lining; watch tucked beneath fabric belt. Columbus, Ohio.

Bodice has small hip flaps and closes at side of plastron. Narrow, black fabric watch chain hangs around neck, with watch positioned beneath side closure. Astoria, Oregon.

Bodice with wide, cape-like bertha and leg-of-mutton sleeves. Minneapolis, Minnesota.

Velvet trims large Vandyke collar, flared mousquetaire cuffs, and hem of tight-fitting bodice. Astoria, Oregon.

Bodice features diagonal closure covered in large part by separate, T-shaped lace collarette. Ashland, Oregon.

Large bertha and mousquetaire cuffs with narrow jet trim. Hair displays prominent top knot. Iron River, Michigan.

The gowns of five of these ladies contain drooping central box pleats. Everyone has short bangs but no top knot. Willmar, Minnesota.

Wedding photo. Turn-down collar fits high on neck. Gigot sleeves; puffed, though not drooping, plastron; wide, flaring mousquetaire cuffs. Prominent hair comb replaces top knot. Georgetown, Colorado.

Fancy tailored suit. Open jacket above figured blouse that has stiff, high-standing, turn-down collar. Island Pond, Vermont.

Very business-like tailored costume, Jacket displays wide revers above blouse or "vest." Drooping balloon sleeves. Boston, Massachusetts.

Very casual pose. Lady wears striped shirt with central drooping box pleat and the huge balloon sleeves popular by 1895-96. Johnsonburg, Pennsylvania.

Blouse with huge balloon sleeves; lace, turn-down collar; puffed but not drooping center. Ventura, California.

Wide assortment of light-colored shirtwaists—many striped, all with turn-down collars—most feature full bishop sleeves and manly neckties. Watches of ladies seated at right are clearly revealed beneath their belts. All ladies have prominent top knots. Martinsville, Illinois.

Very sleek, professional-looking skirt and shirtwaist. Manly neck tie beneath stiff, turn-down collar; large belt buckle. Outline of corset plainly visible beneath shirt. Anoka, Minnesota.

Massive, leg-of-mutton sleeves partially covered by large epaulets ornament fulled, velvet-trimmed blouse. Chicago, Illinois.

Large gigot sleeves; crush collar framed by upright, flaring Medici. Nashville, Tennessee. Hand dated "April, 1896."

WM. HAMEL, FINEST FINISH. STUDIO. 939 ELM STREET, MANCHESTER, N.H.

Turn-down collar above fancy beaded bertha. Manchester, New Hampshire.

Tight-fitting bodice reveals outline of corset beneath. Victoria chain hints at presence of watch, probably hidden within lateral pocket attached near center closure. Simple beaded choker visible above crush collar. Boston, Massachusetts.

Gowns of both ladies feature plastrons and huge balloon sleeves. Hair is simply waved and confined in rear bun. Columbus, Ohio. Hand dated "March, 1896."

Bodice of lady standing hugs mid-section; fulled fabric above fits loosely over hooked inner lining; watch eases between outer fabric and lining. Huge balloon sleeves burden corsage of seated lady. Minneapolis, Minnesota.

Chapter Eighteen

1897-1900

Costumes burdened by overlarge bodice embellishments endured only a few years before sanity once again returned to fashion. Sleeves deflated, leaving a puff as a mere vestige of what had preceded. Skirts diminished as well (though not as dramatically), and hairstyles simplified, losing their distinctive topknot. A more feminine appeal began to replace fashions made ridiculous by exaggeration, and what remained resembled a toned-down version of the preceding period.

Outfits

Bodices retained the focus of attention and were even more inventive and complex. Though some were fashioned from a solid piece of fabric, many featured large cutaway portions. Among other styles they could fasten at the waist, with the entire center cut in a V; over the bust line, forming a low neck with an inverted V below; or at the side and shoulder seam, dipping to a low V, square, or rounded neckline. The contrasting fabric used to fill the gaping areas could be attached to an inner lining or consist of a separate chemisette (or the similar front), blouse, or full sleeveless vest. Fillers became more varied and fanciful in both design and fabric (though plain white was still used). Yokes of contrasting fabric in straight, rounded, scalloped, V, or reverse V shapes were common as well. These generally proved the only interruption to garments that were otherwise constructed from fabrics displaying a single hue or small prints.

While most bodices ended at the waist, some displayed hiplength basques occasionally featuring scalloped hemlines. Though sleeves had become considerably smaller, bodice embellishments like revers and epaulets could still be fairly sizable. Revers might enhance corsages cut in a deep V or become one with epaulettes when framing wide scooped necklines. Lace expanded in usage, softening garments as it enriched collars and cuffs or fell in a distinctive line down one side of the corsage. Braided or jet gimp and passementerie added further ornamentation, edging revers and epaulets or appearing in fanciful designs upon the bodice or skirt. Costumes of elegant silk or brocade often complemented fine trim.

Bodices featuring gathers or pleats at the mid-section became the norm. Sometimes fitting smoothly, they more often produced excess fabric that may or may not droop below the waistline. This fullness, though concentrated mostly at center front, would soon develop into the full-frontal "Kangaroo Pouch" that would help shape the "Gibson Girl's" exaggerated, S-curved silhouette after the turn of the century.

Tailored suits remained popular, and the skirt and blouse became even more prolific. Blouses continued to bear a strong resemblance to bodices, and the two terms became interchangeably used in fashion literature to designate any bodice of a different color and fabric from the skirt. Not content with being stylish for the home and street, they even blossomed into evening attire with elegant trims and low decolletage. A more graceful aspect replaced the professional appeal of the stark blouses and manly neckties displayed by many mid-decade ensembles. Blouses now appeared in a wide assortment of prints and hues that provided a colorful contrast to the accompanying skirt. Often embellished with yokes, tucks, or flounces, they could fasten at the front or side and be worn in or outside the skirt (though the more formal appearance lent by the absence of the lower extremity remained preferred for street attire). Belts could be integral or separate entities and were available in deep or shallow, smooth or crushed versions that frequently featured a large, off-centered bow. Often blouses appeared beneath the increasingly-popular narrow, waist-length bolero vests, which were elegantly fashioned of velvet, silk braid, or jet. Occasionally, they were covered in part by "over blouses" or "waist decorations," which could assume any number of shapes. Formed of fabric, ribbon, or lace (or combinations thereof), these side-less, open-work garnitures extended beyond the shoulders and then narrowed to a plastron or suspender-like design (often repeated at the back), with an attached waistband and optional collar anchoring them to the bodice.

Skirts differed little from those at mid-decade. They were usually cut in gores and fell in a slight triangular shape, only the circumference was somewhat smaller and the plain surfaces were sometimes enhanced with decorative trim. Applied in simple lines or more ornate scallops and loops, trim might appear in a vertical sideline that continued to sweep horizontally across the hem. Skirts remained gathered or pleated in back for extra fullness, but lightweight materials began to replace the stiff, heavy fabrics that had been popular since the eighties. As linings were of softer materials as well, garments flowed more gracefully. The trumpet-shaped skirt was introduced, generally yoked and close-fitting on the upper half and flaring below the knees, where it was sometimes shaped into accordion pleats. The preference remained, however, for the more simple, triangular form—the newer style awaiting the turn of the century before predominating.

Sleeves

The large balloon sleeves of the mid-nineties receded into a small ball placed high on the arm, with the remainder of the snug sleeve covering the wrist. Soon diminishing to a petite "puff," which could alternately appear limp and deflated, the upper arm was usually hidden in part by prominent epaulets—either square, pointed, scalloped, or ruffled—as these had become an especially-popular embellishment. Turned-back cuffs were no longer favored. A fall of lace or a small ruffle often edged the long sleeves, or they could end with a point or flared cuffs that partially hid the hand. Blouses continued to feature the standard bishop along with the more fashionable puff sleeves.

Necklines

Necks were entirely hidden beneath high standing collars, which still fastened at the side or back in plain or crushed versions. Stiff and inflexible (some were even boned), they reached just below the chin, restricting natural head movements and contributing greatly to the solemn, dignified appearance of the wearer. Ample portions of lace might appear from beneath to cradle the chin or fold gracefully down to form a double collar. Along with the newer waist decorations, detachable collars, berthas, and collarettes lingered from mid-decade to enliven a plain bodice or extend the usefulness of a worn-out corsage.

Jewelry

Necks and arms completely encased in fabric left little room for jewels. Except for the thin gold or black fabric watch chain with slide worn around the neck (the watch continuing to repose most often beneath the belt) or the still-popular brooch or bar pin attached at the base of the collar, little jewelry surfaced. The occasional small studs or tiny drop earrings provided the sole brightening to the nineties preference for bare ears.

Hairstyles

Acknowledged even at the time as unflattering to all but the most pleasing of countenances, hair provided little in the way of facial enrichment. The popularity of bangs, top knots, and hair combs was waning. Most styles featured hair simply parted in the middle and worn flat on top. The sides were crimped to form a slight fullness and either partially covered the ears or left them exposed before sweeping into a bun not visible from the front.

Light-colored blouse of lady seated to the left features fancy puffed sleeves; side closure. Bishop sleeves distinguish darker blouse. Both are worn with leather belts, whose popularity since the sixties lagged far behind that of fabric belts. West Superior, Wisconsin.

Full white shirtwaist with large puffed sleeves closes side front and is enhanced by bolero vest flaps and matching, lace-draped collar. Allegan, Michigan.

Large puffed sleeves characteristic of early in the period; side-front closure; pleated mid-section; flared cuffs; crush collar framed by large bow. Neat gores plainly visible on skirt. Hair retains top knot. San Francisco, California.

Full bodice; slightly diminished puff sleeves covered by deep epaulets. Sacramento, California.

W. H. Jones,   Cedar Springs, Mich.

High collar, full bodice, puffed sleeves with lace epaulets, and bolero flaps augment bodice. Cedar Springs, Michigan.

Close-fitting bodice with slightly-puffed plastron and matching striped epaulets. Portland, Oregon.

Wedding photo. Yoked bodice has low ruffled collar, puffed sleeves, and large, off-center bow decorating belt. Redlands, California.

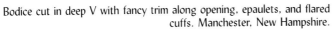

Full blouse with attached bolero flaps and puff sleeves ending in a fall of lace; deep striped belt and collar. NM

Bodice cut in deep V with fancy trim along opening, epaulets, and flared cuffs. Manchester, New Hampshire.

Wedding photo. Bodice cut in deep V; slim-fitting sleeves have puffs and epaulets at shoulders; high standing collar enhanced by overhanging lace. Gored, triangular-shape skirt has line of trim down one side that continues in loops across hem. Lincoln, Nebraska.

Side-front view of preceding garment shows bodice fulled at center and worn above what is probably a fancy, sleeveless vest. Manchester, New Hampshire.

Cutaway bodice worn over simple white blouse or sleeveless vest. Tight sleeves form point at wrist. NM

Wide neckline of bodice combines revers and epaulets; sleeveless, blouse-like vest probably worn underneath. Blue Earth City, Minnesota.

Belt encircles open jacket with puff sleeves and deep revers partially covering what is probably a shirred, fulled vest. NM

Full front worn over bodice. Center parted and waved hair held flat by hair combs. Creston, Iowa.

Simple bodice displays fulled fabric center front. A fall of lace enhances side-front closure and sleeve hem; large side bow on belt. Wahoo, Nebraska.

Elegant cutaway bodice worn over beaded blouse or vest. Fancy puffed and ruffled sleeves. Narrow watch chain around neck. Oakland, California.

Fulled blouses droop center front and feature flounces or gimp trim. Bodice of lady seated on floor has deep V opening, filled by what is probably a vest featuring horizontal tucks. Astoria, Oregon.

Elegant bodice enhanced by T-shaped lace collarette. Watch appears to be tucked beneath tight-fitting mid-section of bodice. Fancy comb tops waved hair. Binghampton, New York.

Rich fulled blouse with puffed sleeves. Lace hangs above deep collar and beneath sleeves. Thin watch chain around neck; watch disappears beneath belt, which is embellished by popular side bow. Manchester, New Hampshire.

Jacket features wide revers garnished by scrolled gimp. Separate vest or blouse has one-sided lace trim. Large side bow at waist. Frankinville, New York.

BRADBROOK & WEGMANN,

Moon Block Gallery,   Red Cloud, Nebraska.

Skirt of seated woman displays fancy jet trim proceeding upward from hem. Large bar pin rests at base of collar, which is overhung by black lace. Red Cloud, Nebraska.

Wedding photo. Fancy scalloped trim enhances bodice, whose modest puffed sleeves are almost hidden by large epaulets. Typical large bow featured on belt. New Ulm, Minnesota.

Fancy cutaway bodice sports large revers and deflated puffs; beautifully-figured vest or blouse rests beneath. Hair retains top knot. Park city, Utah.

Bodice fulled in center and droops below satin belt with large side bow; large epaulets surmount deflated puffs; fancy jet bolero vest. San Francisco, California. Photo imprinted "1899."

Rare "waist decoration" fits over fulled bodice and is anchored by belt and collar. Allentown, Pennsylvania.

V-shaped bodice with large epaulets and deflated puffs; huge bow placed side front of belt; horizontal skirt trim repeated on bodice. Logan, Kansas.

Wide bodice neckline combines revers and epaulets. Fancy, crochet-covered vest or blouse enhanced by dark fabric watch chain; watch peeks above large bow on belt. Fancy scalloped trim along skirt hem repeated on bodice. Reading, Pennsylvania.

Both ladies wear similar basques augmented by epaulets and opening in a deep V at front. Minneapolis, Minnesota.

Corsage features scalloped basque, revers, and epaulets. Skirt decorated with vertical and horizontal trim. Du Quoin, Illinois. Hand dated "February, 1900."

Appendix

Dating the Victorian Paper Photograph

Knowledge of women's ever-changing fashions provides the best tool for dating studio (and historic) photographs. The subtle changes that took place throughout the nineteenth century in card stock, studio settings, and photographer's imprints can also be a valuable aid in determining the age of studio photographs (especially those lacking a woman's presence). (Note: If a photograph displays one or two characteristics of a preceding or succeeding period, it is a good indication the picture dates toward the beginning or end (as applicable) of the interval.)

1860-1864

Pose

Women stood to the side and behind a myriad of different fancy chairs, with one hand resting on the corner of their wooden crest. Less often, they were posed next to a balustrade or seated in a chair beside a table. When couples were present, the woman stood rather stiffly next to the seated gentleman, sometimes with one hand upon his shoulder. The use of head clamps to prevent movement during the fifteen to thirty second exposure times may explain why, in the age of chivalry, gentlemen remained seated while ladies stood—as their skirts effectively hid the unsightly base of the stand.

Setting

A curtain variously draped at one side was common, as were carpets with large geometric or flowered designs. Though plain backgrounds predominated, painted backdrops of windows and drapes or a scene depicting classical ruins occasionally appeared—both having been common in painted portraits for the past century. While scenic backdrops lent a vague feeling of being outdoors, they achieved little realism when coupled with fancy chairs, carpets, and drapes. Furniture utilized as props mirrored the styles currently fashionable—which for the sixties meant, in order of preference—Rococo, Renaissance, and Gothic.

Card Stock

The carte de visite (or "CDV," 2 3/8" x 4"), so named as it was sometimes left in place of calling cards when visiting, was invented in Europe in 1854 and introduced to America around 1859. Made from thin, easily bendable white card stock squared at the corners, CDVs were typically edged by double lines of gold (or sometimes red or blue), the outer line generally thicker. Occasionally a borderless, slightly thicker and larger card (measuring up to 2 1/2" x 4 3/8") was utilized. Some photographs had a stamp placed on the reverse side, indicating payment of the tax levied upon them by the Federal Government between August 1864 and August 1866.

Photographer's Imprint

The photographer's name and location appeared in small black print (though red, brown, purple, and blue were also used) at the center back of the picture, sometimes within a small circle or fancy cartouche. On rare occasions, it could appear instead at the forefront.

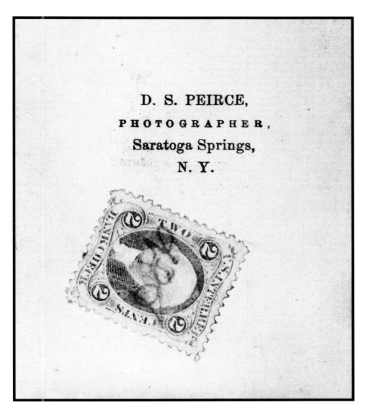

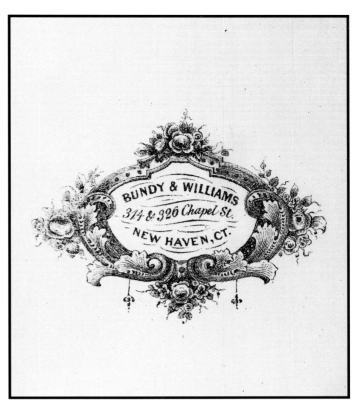

Photographer's name and location written in small black print and centered upon the back of the card—typical throughout the sixties. Presence of a tax stamp indicates picture was taken between August 1864 and August 1866.

Photographer's identification written within fancy cartouche—another popular sixties format.

1865-1868

Pose
Women remained standing next to chairs, balustrades, or their seated husbands.

Setting
Side curtains, patterned carpets, and plain backgrounds occasionally interrupted by painted backdrops continued to prevail. Though "outdoor" scenes remained scarce, depictions of natural foliage began to emerge. A simple, armless chair probably made specifically for photographic studios competed with Rococo, Renaissance, and Gothic styles. Here women were often seated sideways, with one arm resting upon its fringed backrest.

Card Stock
Square cartes de viste surrounded by double lines continued to predominate, supplemented by the slightly larger and thicker borderless format. Shiny "enameled" cards made an occasional appearance. The larger cabinet size (4 1/4" x 6 1/2"), though developed in England in 1863 and available in America three years later, would not see widespread use until the following period.

Photographer's Imprint
The photographer's identification remained compactly printed within an occasional circle or cartouche, though a few were only vaguely discernible impressed into the bottom of the card. Scalloped lines composing a loosely-shaped diamond, often with a diaper pattern outside, enclosed some imprints.

Along with the photographer's identification written simply or enclosed within a fancy cartouche, from the mid- to late-sixties it could appear within scalloped lines composing a loosely-shaped diamond, often with a diaper pattern outside.

Pose

A chair introduced to photographic studios in the mid-sixties became especially popular during the seventies, its use declining gradually through the eighties. It was tall and fully upholstered except for stubby wooden legs partially hidden by long fringe, and the top curved into a backward roll sporting large side tassels. Women were often found standing behind this chair, leaning slightly forward as they rested their folded arms upon its comfortable back. In the less common seated pose, they usually had one or both arms resting upon a table or the upholstered, fringed back of the smaller photographer's chair, toward which they leaned slightly. Women were often posed from the side to take full advantage of their bustled garment's luxuriant folds, displayed in greater detail by the popular three-quarter length views. When standing next to a seated gentleman, one arm generally rested familiarly upon his shoulder. Women's stance appeared more graceful and their countenances more relaxed than in other decades—with lips sometimes forming just a hint of a smile. Long exposure times, though trying, were not necessarily responsible for solemn expressions, as features were far more natural and at-ease during the early seventies than the nineties, when instantaneous photos were possible. (More likely, it suited the formal nature of the entire period to appear as distinguished as possible for one's portrait.)

Setting

Curtains still appeared at the side of many photographs, often casually extended upon chairs and tables. Balustrades were rarely seen, and unpatterned carpets predominated. The majority of photographs had plain backgrounds. At most, a painted backdrop depicted the blurry edge of a window, fireplace, or mammoth piece of furniture. Outdoor scenes were rare. Chairs (besides the upholstered one described above) and the rare exposed tables were in the preferred Renaissance style of the seventies.

Card Stock

Cabinets as well as CDVs (now standardized to 2 1/2" x 4 1/8") were favored. Two other sizes were introduced: the Victoria (3 1/4" x 5") and the Promenade (3 3/4" x 7 1/2")—though the popularity of these and future sizes would be insignificant compared with that of the CDV (at least until the early eighties) and cabinet. Card stock was thicker and usually rounded at the corners. Pale orange was favored with white, tan, and pale yellow also used. Often, a single thin gold line surrounded the picture, equidistantly placed between the edge of the photo and card. With the popularity of the larger cabinet card facial flaws became more apparent, and by 1869 negatives were being retouched to remove wrinkles, moles, and other imperfections.

Photographer's Imprint

The print was larger and fancier, written in red and gold as well as black and often encompassing the entire card back. Though usually placed horizontally, it could also appear vertically or diagonally or be incorporated within an often-elaborate banner, medallion, or shield. The photographer's name and location could be limited to the front or back or appear simultaneously upon both.

Throughout the seventies and to a lesser degree the eighties, print becomes larger and fancier, written horizontally, vertically, or diagonally across the card back.

Photographer's name and location might be incorporated within an elaborate banner, medallion, or shield during the seventies and early eighties.

1876-1878

Pose

Women generally stood straight (the slight lean less favored now) behind a chair or, less often, beside a large cement pillar (for the "outdoor" scenes), hands resting at the top. The overall stance was more serious than the previous period, with fewer hints at a smile, and would remain so throughout the century. Couple's photographs were of a more intimate nature, with the man sitting while the woman gently, trustingly rested one arm on his shoulder and the other upon his arm. Side poses remained popular, affording a better look at the luxuriant trains, which were nicely accommodated by the full-length views again prevailing.

Setting

Hazy "outdoor" scenes grew in popularity, with increased usage of "grass" and "flowers" strewn upon the floor enhancing the "nature" effect. Otherwise, plain backgrounds or blurred windows and fireplaces continued to dominate, accompanied by Renaissance furniture frequently draped by the ever-popular side curtains.

Card Stock

Cabinets and CDVs were both popular. White card stock returned to ascendancy, accompanied by a few lingering yellows, tans, and oranges. Pastels began to appear in green and gray, with light blue, pink, or yellow sometimes featured at the back of white cards. While square-cornered cards existed through the end of the century, most were rounded. The Boudoir, a large print 5 1/4" x 8 1/2", was introduced at the end of this period. Some photographs appeared "framed" within an arch, or, less often, a circle.

Photographer's Imprint

Fancifully-scrolled print positioned horizontally, vertically, or diagonally upon most of the card back continued, with banners, medallions, and shields also remaining popular.

1879-1882

Pose

When posed as a couple, the woman's hand or forearm that rested upon her seated husband's shoulder did so casually rather than intimately. Otherwise, chair backs, cement pillars, and urns provided the convenient resting place.

Setting

Plain backgrounds became the exception, with more detailed, but still indistinct, in- or outdoor scenes the rule. Furniture was in the Renaissance or newly-emerging Eastlake style. Though less often obscured by curtains, it could be burdened with separate fabric throws.

Card Stock

White cards maintained their popularity, with pastels lingering on some backs. Orange cards vanished. The simulated arch and circle were seldom featured. Thick gold borders, which saw sporadic use during the seventies, became more popular, and beveled edges emerged, frequently highlighted with gold. The long, narrow Panel Print (4" x 8 1/4") was introduced.

Photographer's Imprint

Along with shields, medallions, and large, fanciful print, a few cards began to feature elaborate borders and designs often incorporating Japanese or Egyptian motifs.

In addition to large fanciful print sometimes incorporated within medallions or shields, cards during the eighties exhibit oriental influences. This card pictures bamboo, a stork, and the rising sun.

1883-1888

Pose

Women continued to pose standing or, less often, seated, with hands resting upon the standard objects, and it was becoming more common to photograph several people together. The typical dignified appearance somewhat eased in group pictures, occasionally approaching levity. Pictures of couples were less intimate, often displaying no physical contact. While bustles were once again popular, side poses were scarce. Head and shoulder views, used in all periods to a lesser extent, now through the early nineties might appear within a scroll or other decorative effect.

Setting

Along with blurry in- or outdoor scenes, clearly focused, intricately-painted backdrops appeared. "Outdoor" scenes exhibited more realistic depictions of trees, foliage, and buildings. Interiors featured doorways in addition to windows and perhaps a staircase or larger, more distinct portion of the usual fireplace. As in the homes of the eighties, dado or frieze wallpapers adorned with framed pictures might divide "walls"—conferring the impression of an actual dwelling rather than a photographic studio. The Eastlake chairs and tables that dominated private homes were standard. Plain backdrops became scarce.

Card Stock

From this time forward, CDVs were seldom used, their popularity far exceeded by the cabinet card. White card stock appeared with the greatest frequency, followed by dark brown, wine, dark green, and black. Dark colored cards were usually a light gray on the reverse, and pink still occurred on the backs of a few white cards. Beveled edges, often enhanced with gold, occurred as often as straight.

Photographer's Imprint

Though some cards continued to feature large fanciful script or Japanese (the Egyptian less-favored) designs, most simply displayed the photographer's name and location beneath the picture. More photographers utilized the reverse for advertising (done previously to a small extent), proudly announcing their pictures were taken with the aid of the electric light or the new "instantaneous" process. Those fortunate enough to have access to one or both inventions made sure potential customers were aware, as they viewed cards of friends and family, that as long as their establishment was frequented, long exposure times and fair weather were no longer requisite. These developments were not without their drawbacks. The instantaneous process—made possible by the practical use of the dry plate around 1883—was expensive, and many photographers did not have the means to take advantage of its three-second exposure times (as the lingering presence of head clamps in assorted photos from the eighties and early nineties attests). Photographers could not yet relinquish their upper-story studios either, much to the dismay of their clients, who arrived rather disheveled after climbing numerous flights of stairs. Early forms of Edison's 1879 invention often proved unreliable, and the sunlight pouring through studio skylights provided necessary backup to the electric light.

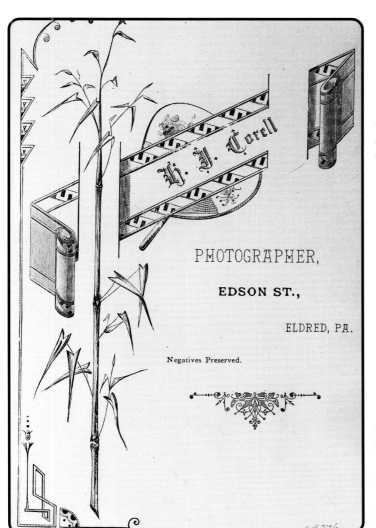

The Japanese influence lingers throughout the eighties—this card featuring bamboo and an oriental fan.

Though most cards relegate the photographer's identification beneath the picture at the bottom front, a few picturesquely display such items as an artist's pallet on the reverse. Card backs were also used to advertise the use of such innovations as the "instantaneous process."

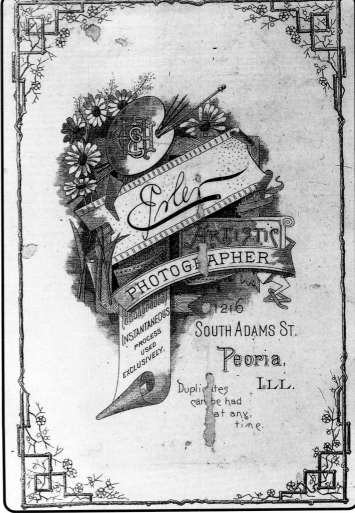

Pose

As instantaneous photos no longer required props for steadiness, women often stood with their arms hanging straight at their sides or with folded hands resting on their stomach or behind their back. Shorter exposure times also freed men to stand as well as sit. When photographed together stiff formality continued to prevail, and a common stance featured arms awkwardly linked. The disappearance of the bustle ushered the demise of the side pose.

Setting

Backdrops, either focused or hazy, remain fairly detailed. While the use of side curtains declined during the eighties, the prolific doorway portieres from that period began to infiltrate a few photos of the nineties (in actual or painted versions).

Card Stock

Cabinet cards predominated. Cards were now the same color, front and back, with white used almost exclusively. A thin gold line often surrounded the card, and straight, beveled, and serrated edges were all popular—the later becoming squared at the corners.

Photographer's Imprint

The photographer's identification appeared in gold ink or colorlessly impressed upon the photo. While most cards remained simply imprinted on the front, elaborate designs (lacking the oriental influence) lingered upon a few. Females, cupids, or photographic and artistic equipment (the later portrayed to a small extent since the sixties) prevailed. Artists' pallets and brushes were most common, as enhancing pictures with color was possible throughout the period of paper photography—either completely or, more often, to emphasize jewelry or add a rosy hue to cheeks or lips. Photographs could also be enlarged and either colored over the top with charcoal or pastels or painted with watercolors or oils, thereby creating a very realistic and true-to-life work of art.

With the oriental influence lessening, some cards feature elaborate flower motifs often incorporating females or cupids (though the majority remain simply imprinted at the card front).

Opposite Page

Though used to a limited extent since the sixties, elaborate depictions of photographic and artistic equipment increase during the early nineties.

Pose

Women and men continued to pose interchangeably seated or standing. Despite the now-common shortened exposure times, facial expressions remained solemn or just on the verge of a smile, though group pictures displayed more levity than in previous decades.

Setting

Focused and blurred backdrops were becoming less detailed, with "outdoor" scenes preferred; furniture for both was almost exclusively wicker or rattan. The animal-skin rugs thrown haphazardly upon household floors were now featured prominently underfoot. With the exception of a few table covers, fabric throws rarely obscured furniture.

Card Stock

A great variety of sizes, large and small, were available, but the cabinet remained most favored. White card stock was used almost exclusively, still frequently bordered by a narrow gold line. Serrated edges were losing their appeal. A new innovation featured impressed geometric designs molded into the face of the card.

Photographer's Imprint

Though elaborate drawings still appeared on the backs of a few cards, most had their fronts alone colorlessly impressed or simply imprinted in gold or reddish-brown ink with the photographer's identification.

An especially elaborate card back from the mid-nineties with cupids, birds, photographic equipment, and fancy print.

Most cards are simply imprinted at the bottom front, though a few retain their elaborate drawings of females, cupids, or photographic equipment.

1897-1900

Pose
Women remained stiffly standing or seated beside their husbands or tables.

Setting
Wicker furniture and animal-skin rugs set before simple in- or outdoor backdrops continued to prevail.

Card Stock
Serrated edges and molded geometric designs were no longer fashionable. Beveled edges were still used, though generally lacking the enhancement of gold highlighting. While white cabinet cards predominated, light and dark gray began to vie in popularity. (By the turn of the century, dark gray would prevail in a myriad of different sizes that would soon mark the demise of the fashionable Victorian cabinet card.)

Photographer's Imprint
Most cards had plain backs, with photographers' names and locations restricted to the forefront, either impressed or printed in assorted colors.

Price Guide

Photographs

Photographs picturing ordinary Victorians (such as appear in the bulk of this book) are considered common. Prices range anywhere from fifty cents to eight dollars, depending on the dealer.

Vintage Clothing

As a courtesy to collectors of vintage clothing, a price guide is included. This guide is only meant to give a general idea of value. The pricing of any antique is not an exact science, and is influenced by many factors. Dealers do not have a standard supply source. They buy largely from unpredictable auctions or the general public, and the price paid to either can fluctuate considerably, influencing what the dealer may then have to charge. Prices vary greatly from one part of the country to another due to the scarcity and desirability of a particular object. Age, material, trim, the presence of an overskirt or train, rarity for the time period, and condition also affect the price of clothing. (In general, the more elaborate the piece, the more expensive. The possible exception to this would be 1860s gowns, which are slightly more prized, despite their relative simplicity, due to their value to Civil War re-enactors.) Estimates of gown values taken from photographs must from necessity be generalized, as materials are guessed at and the backs and inner construction of gowns unseen. I have not attempted to price clothing unless the entire front is visible. The outfit alone is priced—accessories such as hats, outer wraps, shawls, fichus, cravats, etc., are not included. Prices shown assume clothing is in excellent condition, having no noticeable flaws. Neither the author nor publisher accept responsibility for any outcomes that may result from using this price list.

Chapter 10

1. n/a, p. 43
2. 450, L, p. 44
3. 400, R
4. 200, p. 45
5. 225, BL, p. 46
6. 300, TR
7. 500, BR
8. 375, TL, p. 47
9. 375, BL
10. 525, R
11. 350, L, p. 48
12. 500, R
13. 450, L, p. 49
14. n/a, R
15. 300, TL, p. 50
16. 325, TR
17. 325, BL
18. 300, BR
19. 350, L, p. 51
20. 225, TR
21. 350, BR
22. 500, p. 52

23. 475, TL, p. 53
24. 475, BL
25. 300, TR
26. 250, BR
27. n/a, TL, p. 54
28. 400, R
29. 350, BL
30. 400, TL, p. 55
31. n/a, R
32. 400, BL
33. n/a, TL, p. 56
34. 275, TR
35. 250, BL
36. 200, BR
37. n/a, TL, p. 57
38. 375, BL
39. 375, TR
40. n/a, BR

Chapter 11

1. n/a, p. 58
2. 300, p. 59
3. 350, T, p. 60

4. 350, B
5. n/a, L, p. 61
6. 300, TR
7. 425, BR
8. n/a, TL, p. 62
9. 350, BR
10. 350, L, p. 63
11. 300, R
12. n/a, L, p. 64
13. 300, TR
14. 450, BR
15. 350, L, p. 65
16. 350, R
17. n/a, L, p. 66
18. 375, R
19. 350, TL, p. 67
20. n/a, BL
21. 250, R
22. 375, L, p. 68
23. n/a, R
24. 325, L, p. 69
25. n/a, R
26. n/a, TL, p. 70
27. 325, C

28. 325, BL
29. 525, p. 71
30. 325, BR, p. 70
31. 450, TR

Chapter 12

1. n/a, p. 72
2. 450, p. 73
3. 425, T, p. 74
4. n/a, B
5. 450, L, p. 75
6. 350, C
7. 375, R
8. 300, TL, p. 76
9. n/a, TR
10. 450, BL
11. 350, BR
12. 475, L, p. 77
13. n/a, R
14. 425, L, p. 78
15. 475, R
16. n/a, p. 79
17. 550, TL, p. 80

18. n/a, TR
19. n/a, BL
20. 550, BR
21. 500, TL, p. 81
22. n/a, TR
23. 375, BL
24. 450, BR
25. n/a, TL, p. 82
26. n/a, TR
27. n/a, BL
28. n/a, BR
29. n/a, TL, p. 83
30. n/a, TR
31. n/a, BL
32. n/a, BR
33. 450, TL, p. 84
34. n/a, TR
35. n/a, BL
36. n/a, BR
37. n/a, TL, p. 85
38. 675, BL
39. 550, R

Chapter 13

1. n/a, p. 86
2. 375, L, p. 87
3. 475, R
4. 400, T, p. 88
5. 425, C
6. 475, B
7. 425, L, p. 89
8. 550, R
9. n/a, p. 90
10. 425, TL, p. 91
11. 425, BL
12. n/a, R
13. 550, L, p. 92
14. 550, TR
15. 300, BR
16. n/a, L, p. 93
17. 475, R
18. 575, L, p. 94
19. 550, R
20. 450, L, p. 95
21. 450, TR
22. 475, BR
23. 475, TL, p. 96
24. 425, TR
25. 650, BL
26. n/a, L, p. 97
27. n/a, TR
28. 650, BR
29. 500, L, p. 98
30. 500, R
31. n/a, TL, p. 99
32. 550, TR
33. 475, BL
34. 500, BR

Chapter 14

1. n/a, p. 100
2. 650, T, p. 101
3. n/a, C
4. 450, B
5. n/a, T, p. 102
6. n/a, C

7. n/a, B
8. 450, L, p. 103
9. 450, R
10. 425, T, p. 104
11. 450, BR
12. n/a, BL
13. 450, p. 105
14. 650, p. 106
15. 600, TL, p. 107
16. 600, C
17. 450, BR
18. 450, L, p. 108
19. 525, R
20. 675, p. 109
21. 300, TL, p. 110
22. 375, TR
23. 800, BL
24. n/a, TL, p. 111
25. 600, TR
26. 650, BL
27. n/a, BR
28. n/a, TL, p. 112
29. n/a, TR
30. n/a, B
31. 450, L, p. 113
32. 425, R
33. 525, TL, p. 114
34. n/a, BL
35. 775, TR
36. n/a, BR
37. 525, TL, p. 115
38. 475, R
39. 700, BL
40. 700, p. 116
41. 400, TL, p. 117
42. n/a, BL
43. n/a, R

Chapter 15

1. n/a, p. 118
2. 450, L, p. 119
3. 425, R
4. n/a, TR, p. 120
5. 425, BL
6. 475, BR
7. 450, L, p. 121
8. 450, R
9. 525, L, p. 122
10. 600, R
11. 550, L, p. 123
12. n/a, R
13. 550, p. 124
14. 425, p. 125
15. 600, L, p. 126
16. 525, R
17. 400, TL, p. 127
18. 300, CL
19. 425, TR
20. 425, CR
21. n/a, BL
22. 475, BR
23. n/a, TL, p. 128
24. 600, TR
25. n/a, BL
26. 500, BR
27. n/a, L, p. 129
28. 475, R

29. n/a, L, p. 130
30. n/a, R
31. 475, L, p. 131
32. n/a, R

Chapter 16

1. n/a, p. 132
2. n/a, L, p. 133
3. n/a, R
4. 250, L, p. 134
5. 350, R
6. 325, T, p. 135
7. 325, B
8. 350, L, p. 136
9. n/a, R
10. 200, TL, p. 137
11. 350, TR
12. 225, BL
13. 325, BR
14. n/a, TL, p. 138
15. 350, TR
16. 325, BL
17. 375, BR
18. 325, TL, p. 139
19. 425, TR
20. n/a, BL
21. n/a, BR
22. 250, TL, p. 140
23. 350, CL
24. n/a, R
25. 375, BL
26. 325, TL, p. 141
27. 450, CL
28. 350, BR
29. 375, BL
30. n/a, TR
31. 400, CR

Chapter 17

1. n/a, p. 142
2. 350, L, 143
3. 325, R
4. 350, L, p. 144
5. n/a, R
6. n/a, L, p. 145
7. n/a, R
8. 350, TL, p. 146
9. 425, BL
10. 325, TR
11. 300, TL, p. 147
12. 350, R
13. n/a, BL
14. 400, TL, p. 148
15. n/a, TC
16. n/a, B
17. 400, TR
18. 450, TL, p. 149
19. 300, TR
20. 325, TC
21. 250, B
22. 250, TL, p. 150
23. n/a, TR
24. 175, BL
25. n/a, BR
26. n/a, TL, p. 151
27. n/a, C

28. n/a, BR
29. n/a, BL
30. n/a, TR

Chapter 18

1. n/a, p. 153
2. 250, TL, p. 154
3. n/a, TR
4. 300, BL
5. 250, BR
6. n/a, TL, p. 155
7. 275, TR
8. n/a, BL
9. 325, BR
10. 325, TL, p. 156
11. 375, TR
12. 350, BL
13. 300, BR
14. 300, TL, p. 157
15. 300, TR
16. 275, BR
17. 500, BL
18. n/a, TL, p. 158
19. n/a, TR
20. 325, BL
21. n/a, BR
22. n/a, TL, p. 159
23. n/a, TR
24. 375, BL
25. n/a, BR
26. n/a, L, p. 160
27. 350, R
28. 350, L, p. 161
29. n/a, TR
30. 375, BR

ibliography

Arnold, Janet. *Patterns of Fashion 2: Englishwomen's Dresses and Their Construction, c. 1860-1940*. London: Macmillan; New York: Drama Book Publishers, 2d ed., 1977.

Balderston, Lydia. *Housewifery: A Manual and Text Book of Practical Housekeeping*. Philadelphia: J. B. Lippincott Company, 1919.

Beecher, Catherine E., and Harriet Beecher Stowe. *The American Woman's Home*. 1869. Reprint, New York: American Life Foundation, 1979.

Bell, C. Jeanenne. *Answers to Questions about Old Jewelry, "1840-1950."* Florence, Al: Books Americana, 4th ed., 1996.

Bloomingdale Brothers. *Bloomingdale's Illustrated 1886 Catalog: Fashions, Dry Goods and Housewares*. 1886. With an introduction by Nancy Villa Bryk. Reprint, New York: Dover Publications, 1988.

Blum, Stella, ed. *Fashions and Costumes from Godey's Lady's Book*. New York: Dover Publications, 1985.

_____. *Paris Fashions of the 1890s*. New York: Dover Publications, 1984.

_____. *Victorian Fashions and Costumes from Harper's Bazar, 1867-1898*. New York: Dover Publications, 1974.

Bradfield, Nancy. *Costume in Detail, 1730-1930*. New York: Quite Specific Media Group, Ltd., Costume & Fashion Press, 1997.

Bryk, Nancy V., ed. *American Dress Pattern Catalogs, 1873-1909: Four Complete Reprints*. New York: Dover Publications, 1988.

Burgess, Janet. *Clothing Guidelines for the Civil War Era*. Davenport, IA: Amazon Drygoods, Rev. ed., 1985.

Butterick's 1892 Metropolitan Fashions, The Butterick Publishing Co. With an introduction by Stella Blum. New York: Dover Publications, 1994.

Chesterfield's Art of Letter-Writing Simplified . . . To Which is Appended The Complete Rules of Etiquette and The Usages of Society . . . . New York: Dick & Fitzgerald, 1857.

Civil War Era Etiquette: Martine's Handbook and Vulgarisms in Conversation. 1866 & 1864. Reprint, Mendocino, CA: R. L. Shep, 1988.

Cunnington, C. Willett. *English Women's Clothing in the Nineteenth Century*. 1937. Reprint, New York: Dover Publications, 1990.

Cunnington, C. Willett, and Phillis Cunnington. *The History of Underclothes*. 1951. Reprint, New York: Dover Publications, 1992.

Dalrymple, Priscilla H. *American Victorian Costume in Early Photographs*. New York: Dover Publications, 1991.

Decorum: A Practical Treatise on Etiquette and Dress of the Best American Society. Chicago: J. A. Ruth & Co., 1877.

Domestic Paper Fashions, catalog. New York: Domestic Fashion Co., c. 1880.

Downing, A. J. *The Architecture of Country Houses*. 1850. Reprint, New York: Dover Publications, 1969.

Fowler, C. H., and W. H. De Puy. *Home and Health and Home Economics: A Cyclopedia of Facts and Hints for All Departments of Home Life, Health, and Domestic Economy*. New York: Phillips & Hunt, 1880.

Fowler, Orson S. *The Octagon House: A Home for All*. 1853. Reprint, New York: Dover Publications, 1973.

Gernsheim, Alison. *Victorian and Edwardian Fashion: A Photographic Survey*. New York: Dover Publications, 1963.

Gilbert, George. *Photography: The Early Years*. New York: Harper & Row, 1980.

Green, Harvey. *The Light of the Home: An Intimate View of the Lives of Women in Victorian America*. New York: Pantheon Books, 1983.

Habits of Good Society: A Handbook for Ladies and Gentlemen. New York: Carleton, 1873.

Haines, T. L., and L. W. Yaggy. *The Royal Path of Life: or, Aims and Aids to Success and Happiness*. Sacramento: Eureka Publishing House, 1879.

Hall, W. W., M.D. *Health at Home, or Hall's Family Doctor*. Hartford, CT: James Betts & Co., 1876.

Hartley, Florence. *The Ladies' Book of Etiquette and Manual of Politeness*. Boston: J. S. Locke & Co., 1873.

Hartshorne, Henry, M.D. *The Practical Household Physician: A Cyclopedia of Family Medicine, Surgery, Nursing and Hygiene . . . .* Philadelphia: John C. Winston & Co., Rev. ed., 1891.

Henisch, Heinz K., and Bridget A. Henisch. *The Photographic Experience, 1839-1914*. University Park, PA: The Pennsylvania State University Press, 1994.

Hill, May B. "Making a Virtue of Necessity: Decorative American Privies." *The Magazine Antiques* 154, no. 2 (1998): 182-189.

Holly, Hudson H. *Country Seats and Modern Dwellings: Two Victorian Domestic Architectural Stylebooks by Henry Hudson Holly*. 1863 & 1878. With Introduction by Michael Tomlan. Reprint, New York: American Life Foundation, 1977.

Home Guide, The: A Compendium of Useful Information Pertaining to Every Branch of Domestic and Social Economy. Chicago: J. Fairbanks & Co., 1878.

Israel, Fred. L., ed. *1897 Sears Roebuck Catalog*. 1897. Reprint, New York: Chelsea House Publishers, 1968.

Kalman, Bobbie. *Early Health and Medicine*. New York: Crabtree Publishing Co., 1991.

Kellogg, J.H., M.D. *Ladies' Guide in Health and Disease*. Oakland, CA: Pacific Press Publishing House, 1888.

Kliot, Jules, and Kaethe Kliot, eds. *Garment Patterns, 1889, with*

Instructions. Reprint, Berkely, CA: Lacis Publications, 1996.

Lansdell, Avril. *Fashion à la Carte, 1860-1900.* Bucks, England: Shire Publications, Ltd., 1985.

Leisch, Juanita. *The Family Album: Ladies' Wear Daily.* N.p., Rev. and enl., 1988.

_____. *Who Wore What?: Women's Wear, 1861-1865.* Gettysburg, PA: Thomas Publications, 1995.

Mace, O. Henry. *Collector's Guide to Early Photographs.* Radnor, PA: Wallace-Homestead Book Co., 1990.

Mayhew, Edgar de N., and Minor Myers, Jr. *A Documentary History of American Interiors.* New York: Charles Scribner's Sons, 1980.

McCulloch, Lou W. *Card Photographs, A Guide to their History and Value.* Exton, PA: Schiffer Publishing Ltd., 1981.

Melendy, Mary R., M.D. *Vivilore: The Pathway to Mental and Physical Perfection.* N.p.: W. R. Vansant, 1904.

Metropolitan Fashions of the 1880s, From the 1885 Butterick Catalog. New York: Dover Publications, 1997.

Miller, Annie J. *Physical Beauty: How to Obtain and How to Preserve It.* New York: Charles L. Webster & Co., 1892.

Mills, Betty J. *Calico Chronicle: Texas Women and Their Fashions, 1830-1910.* Lubbock, Texas: Texas Tech Press, 1985.

Mitchell, Eugene, comp. *American Victoriana.* San Francisco: Chronicle Books, 1979.

Montgomery Ward and Co., Catalogue and Buyers' Guide. 1895. With Introduction by Boris Emmet. Reprint, Dover Publica tions, 1969.

Olian, JoAnne, ed. *Wedding Fashions, 1862-1912: 380 Costume Designs from "La Mode Illustrée."* New York: Dover Publications, 1994.

Parloa, Maria. *Home Economics.* New York: The Century Co., 1898.

Picken, Mary B. *The Fashion Dictionary.* New York: Funk & Wagnalls, 1957.

Pierce, R.V., M.D. *The People's Common Sense Medical Adviser in Plain English; or, Medicine Simplified.* Buffalo, NY: World's Dispensary Printing Office & Bindery, 59th ed., 1895.

Rayne, Mrs. M. L. *Gems of Deportment and Hints of Etiquette . . . .* Detroit: Tyler & Co., 1881.

Schroeder, Joseph J., Jr., ed. *1896 Illustrated Catalogue of Jewelry and European Fashions: Marshall Field and Co.* 1896. Reprint, Chicago: Follett Publishing Co., 1970.

_____. *The Wonderful World of Ladies' Fashion, 1850-1920.* Chicago: Follett Publishing Co., 1971

Severa, Joan. *Dressed for the Photographer: Ordinary Americans and Fashion, 1840-1900.* Kent, Ohio: The Kent State University Press, 1995.

Sloan, Samuel. *Sloan's Victorian Buildings: Illustrations of and Floor Plans for 56 Residences and Other Structures* (Originally titled *"The Model Architect"*). 1852. Reprint, New York: Dover Publications, 1980.

Snyder-Haug, Diane. *Antique and Vintage Clothing: A Guide to Dating and Valuation of Women's Clothing, 1850-1940.* Paducah, KY: Collector Books, 1997.

Strasser, Susan. *Never Done: A History of American Housework.* New York: Pantheon Books, 1982.

Swenson, Evelyn. *Victoriana Americana.* Matteson, IL: Greatlakes Living Press, 1976.

Tortora, Phyllis G., and Keith Eubank. *Survey of Historic Costume: A History of Western Dress.* New York: Fairchild Publications, 2d ed., 1994.

Ulseth, Hazel, and Helen Shannon. *Victorian Fashions, Volume I, 1880-1890.* Cumberland, MD: Hobby House Press, 1988.

Weinstock Lubin Co. Catalog, The. 1891. Reprint, Sacramento, CA: Sacramento American Revolution Bicentennial Committee, 1975.

Woolson, Abba G., ed. *Dress-Reform: A Series of Lectures Delivered in Boston, on Dress as it Affects the Health of Women.* Boston: Roberts Brothers, 1874.

Wright, Julia M. *The Complete Home: An Encyclopedia of Domestic Life and Affairs.* Philadelphia: J. C. McCurdy & Co., 1879.

Wright, Lawrence. *Clean and Decent: The History of the Bath and Loo.* London: Routledge & Kegan Paul, Rev. ed., 1980.

Young, John H. *Our Deportment, or the Manners, Conduct and Dress of the Most Refined Society . . . .* Detroit: F. B. Dickerson & Co., Rev. ed., 1882.

Magazines

Arthur's Home Magazine (July, 1870).

Delineator, The (October, 1893; May, 1894; April, 1895; January, 1897).

Demorest's Monthly Magazine (April, 1876).

Domestic Monthly, The (November, 1881).

Frank Leslie's Lady's Magazine (February, 1875; July, 1875; August, 1876).

Godey's Lady's Book (Microfilm: 1861-1863; 1866-1883; 1887-1889; 1896; September 1897- December 1897).

Harper's Bazar (March, 1870; December, 1870; November, 1873; July, 1888).

Peterson's Ladies National Magazine (February, 1864; April, 1864; November, 1865; March, 1872; February, 1877; May, 1877; June, 1877; November, 1877).

Young Ladies' Journal (September, 1876).

Index

advertising photographs, 166
alterations, 6, 19
apron drapes (see overskirts)
aprons, 12
archery dress, 14
armscye/armhole, 45, 59, 74, 88, 102, 120, 135
balayeuse, 88, 144
balloon sleeves, 144, 152
bangs, 41, 61, 75, 89, 102, 121, 136, 145, 153
bar pin, 89, 102, 121, 135, 145, 153
basque, 14, 58, 59, 72, 73, 86, 100, 102, 118, 119, 121, 133, 134, 142, 152
bathing, 38-39, 41
bathing costumes, 15, 17
bathrooms, 38-39
beads (see jet beads, passementerie)
bell sleeves, 74
belts, 12, 13, 15, 43, 44, 46, 59, 60, 73, 87, 134, 142, 143, 145, 152, 153
bertha, 20, 144, 153
bicycle outfits, 14
bishop sleeves, 45, 60, 135, 144, 153
Bloomer, Amelia, 14
bloomer costume, 14-15
blouses, 19, 133, 134, 142, 143, 145, 152, 153 (also see shirtwaists)
bodices, 10, 12, 20, 34, 37, 43, 44, 45, 46, 59, 60, 72, 73, 74, 75, 86, 87, 88, 100, 101, 102, 118, 119, 120, 121, 132, 133, 134, 135, 142, 143, 144, 145, 152, 153 (also see basque, cuirass)
bolero vests, 59, 143, 152
boning, bodice, 37, 43, 86, 119, 133, 142, 153
boudoir mount, 165
box pleats, 59, 74, 88, 118, 134, 142, 143
bracelets, 21, 46, 60, 75, 89, 102, 121, 135, 145
braids, 46, 61, 75, 89, 102
bretelles, 143, 145
bridal dresses (see wedding dresses)
brooches, 45, 60, 75, 89, 102, 121, 145, 153
buns, 41, 46, 61, 75, 89, 102, 121, 136, 153
busk, 10
bust, artificial, 10, 119
bustles, 10, 12, 13, 14, 35, 59, 72, 73, 86, 87, 101, 118, 119, 133, 134, 164, 166, 168
Butterick, Ebenezer, 35
cabinet cards, 163, 164, 165, 166, 168, 171
calico, 12, 18, 19
cameos, 46, 48
camisole (see corset cover)
camping attire, 14
carriage attire, 13, 19, 59, 101
carte de visite, 162, 163, 164, 165, 166
casaque, 73, 101
casual dress, 12-13, 43
chatelaine, 145
chemise, 10
chemisette, 43, 44, 45, 59, 74, 102, 119, 133, 135, 142, 152
chignons (see buns)
chokers, 46, 60, 75, 89, 135
cistern, 39
cleanliness (see bathing)
clothing, care of, 6, 37
clothing, manufacture of, 34-35
coat sleeves, 45, 60, 74, 88
coiffures (see listings for individual styles)
collarette, 89, 145, 153
collars (see listings for individual styles)

combination underclothes, 10, 14, 86
combs, hair, 61, 75, 89, 145, 153
common dress, 18-19
corsage (see bodices)
corset cover, 10
corsets, 9-10, 11, 12, 13, 14, 15, 19, 20, 34, 35, 43, 59, 72, 86, 100, 119, 135, 142, 143
corslet, 44
cosmetics, 40-41
cravat, 75
crinolette, 10
crinoline (see hoops)
cuff pin, 89
cuffs (see listings for individual styles)
cuirass bodice, 73, 86, 100, 118
cummerbund (see Swiss belt)
curling irons, 40, 41
cutaway bodices, 152
decolletage, 20, 74, 152
Demorest, Ellen, 35
deodorant, 10, 41
department stores, 35, 143
diamond jewelry, 21
dog collar, 121
Dolly Varden, 74
drawers, 10, 11, 15, 35, 86
dress reform, 14
dress shields, 10
dressmakers, 6, 34-35, 101, 143
dry plate, 166
dyes, clothing, 10, 19
earrings, 40, 60, 75, 89, 102, 121, 135, 145, 153
Eastlake furniture, 165, 166
Edison, Thomas, 166
Egyptian-influenced card stock, 165, 166
elevated skirts (see porte jupe)
empire waistline, 59
enameled cards, 163
engageantes (see undersleeves)
epaulettes, 45, 60, 144, 152
equestrian costume, 15
etiquette books/writers, 6, 12, 20, 39, 40, 59
Eton jackets, 143
Eugenie hairstyle, 61
European dress, 10, 13, 42
evening attire, 21, 43, 45, 46, 59, 74, 101, 120, 145, 152
fans, 20
fan-shaped bodice, 44, 45
fan-shaped skirt, 134, 143
fashion magazines/plates, 6, 13, 18, 19, 34, 35, 40, 42, 43, 44, 45, 118, 143
feathers, 20
fibre chamois, 144
fichu, 102
flowers, 20
fluting irons, 37
Foreign fashions (see European dress)
fraise, 75
fronts, 142
Gabrielle dress (see princess dress)
Garabaldi shirts, 43, 59
garters, 11
gauntlet cuffs, 45
Gibson girl, 152
gigot sleeves (see leg-o-mutton sleeves)
gloves, 21
godets, 143
Godey's Lady's Magazine, 6, 19
gored dresses/skirts, 44, 59, 60, 73, 134, 143
Gothic furniture, 162, 163
gussets, 9
gutta percha, 46
habit shirt (see chemisette)
hair care, 39, 40, 41
hair, false, 40-41, 61, 75
hair jewelry, 46
hair nets, 46
hair oil, 39, 40
hairstyles (see listings for individual styles)
handkerchiefs, 121
Harper's Bazaar, 19
head clamps, 162

health stays, 10
hem protectors, 44, 74, 144
hiking clothes, 14
hoops, 10, 12, 13, 14, 34, 44, 59 (also see bustles)
hose supporters, 11
house dresses, 12-13, 19, 59
Howe, Elias, 34
instantaneous process, 166, 168
ironing, 37, 101
jabots, 89, 102, 121, 145
jackets, 13, 15, 19, 43, 44, 59, 73, 133-134, 142, 143 (also see tailor-made)
Japanese-influenced card stock, 166
jersey, 100, 119
jet beads, 46, 59, 60, 75, 100, 101, 120, 121, 142, 145, 152
jewelry (see listings for individual styles)
Kangaroo pouch, 152
kilting (see listings for individual types of pleats/plaits)
knife pleats, 44, 74, 88, 102, 118, 134
lace, 10, 12, 20, 45, 75, 101, 102, 120, 142, 144, 145, 153, 152
lapels, 74, 142, 143
La Pliante, 143
laundry, 36-37, 101
leg-o-mutton sleeve, 144
leisure wear (see casual dress)
lockets, 5, 89, 121, 145
looped skirts, 59
made-overs (see alterations)
mail order, 35, 46
Marguerite basque, 134
maternity wear, 12
Medici collars, 144
modistes (see dressmakers)
Mother Hubbard (see wrapper)
mountain climbing costume, 14
mourning collars, cuffs, 45
mousquetaire cuffs, 144
neck ties (see cravat)
necklaces, 21, 46, 60, 75, 89, 102, 121, 145
négligé dress, 13, 19
over blouse, 134, 152
overdresses (see casaque, polonaise, redingote)
overskirts, 10, 13, 14, 19, 20, 34, 37, 44, 59, 72, 73, 74, 86, 88, 100, 101, 109, 132, 134, 143
oversleeves, 45
pagoda sleeves, 45, 60, 74
paletots, 59
Pamela sleeves, 45
panel print mount, 165
panniers, 9, 73, 100-101, 119
pantalets, 10
parasols, 40
passementerie, 120, 133, 152
patterns, dress, 19, 34-35
pelerines, 59, 100
peplums, 59, 142
petersham, 87
Peterson's National Magazine, 19
petticoats, 10, 12, 19, 44, 59, 74, 86, 87, 142
photographs, dating of, 162-171
pie-crust frill, 74, 89, 102, 120
piping, 45, 74, 88, 119
placket, 43
plastrons, 19, 73, 88, 100, 101, 119, 120, 121, 133, 135, 142, 143, 145, 153
pleats/plaits (see listings for individual styles)
plumbing, 38-39
pockets, clothing, 44, 88, 101
pockets, watch, 46, 60, 89, 102, 121, 135
polonaise, 73, 74, 86-87, 88, 100, 118, 119, 134
pompadour hairstyle, 145
porte-jupe, 44, 57, 59
postilions, 73, 119, 133
princess dress, 12, 13, 60, 86, 100, 134
princess polonaise, 87
promenade mount, 164
puff sleeve, 152
ready-made clothing, 6, 34, 35, 74

redingote, 73, 119
reform dress, 14
Renaissance furnishings, 162, 163, 164, 165
retouching of photographs, 164
revers, 21, 59, 73, 102, 118, 119, 120, 133, 135, 142, 143, 145, 152
riding costume (see equestrian costume)
ringlets, 46, 61
Rococo furniture, 162, 163
ruches, 74, 88
ruffles, 10, 12, 13, 37, 44, 59, 72, 74, 75, 86, 88, 118, 134, 143
Russian outfits, 134, 141
sacque, 12, 59
sash, 73
sausage curls, 75, 89
seamstress (see dressmakers)
sewer gas, 39
sewers, 39
sewing machine, 34, 35, 60, 74, 101
shawl, 44, 21
shirtwaists, 13, 15, 43, 45, 59, 60, 73, 133, 135, 143 (also see blouses)
skirt elevators, 59, 73-74, 88 (also see porte jupe)
sleeves (see listings for individual styles)
sleeves, hoop for, 144
snoods (see hair net)
Spanish jacket (see bolero)
Spencer, 43
sponge bath (see bathing)
sports clothes, 14-15
stays (see corsets)
stick pins, 145
stockings, 11
suspenders, skirt, 10
Swiss belt, 43, 44, 134
tablier (see overskirt)
taille d' epergne, 75, 102, 121
tailor-made, 119, 133, 143, 145, 152
tax stamps, 162
tea gown (see wrapper)
teeth, care of, 39
tennis costume, 14
tie-backs, 73, 87, 101, 118
tournure (see bustle)
trained dresses, 10, 12, 13, 14, 19, 20, 59, 73-74, 86, 87, 88, 101, 118, 134, 144, 165
traveling costume, 19
trumpet-shape skirt, 152
tunics (see polonaise)
Turkish bath, 39
Turkish costume (see bloomers)
umbrellas (see parasols)
underbodice/underlining, 12, 43, 142, 143
undergarments (see listings for specific styles)
underpants (see drawers)
undersleeves, 10, 43, 45, 60, 88, 144
union suits (see combination undergarments)
Valois collar (see Medici collar)
Vandykes, 59, 88, 144
vestee (see chemisette)
vests, 43, 59, 73, 74, 119, 133, 143, 152
Victoria chain, 135, 145
Victoria mount, 164
waist decorations, 153
waists (see shirtwaists)
walking dresses, 59, 74
washing machines, 36
watch chains, 46, 60, 75, 89, 102, 121, 135, 145, 153
watches, 46, 60, 89, 102, 121, 135, 145, 153
water closet, 38, 39
water heaters, 36, 39
waterfall, clothing, 134
waterfall, hairstyle, 46, 61
watteau pleats, 12
wedding dresses, photos of, 90, 91, 117, 137, 138, 140, 147, 149, 155, 156, 159
wicker furniture, 170, 171
Worth, Charles, 19, 42
wrappers, 12-13, 19, 20, 35
yokes, 12, 59, 74, 134, 142, 145, 152
Zouave jackets, 44, 45, 59